Victorian Architect
SECOND EDITION

STORIES AND PHOTOGRAPHS
by William Plymat Jr.

Copyright 1997
Palladian Publishing Company
Des Moines, Iowa

Printed At
Sutherland Companies
Montezuma, Iowa

ISBN 0-9661440-0-7 (paperbound)
ISBN 0-9661440-1-5 (hardcover)

INTRODUCTION

In 1975 I traveled the state of Iowa looking for Victorian buildings to photograph. There were very few reference materials available to indicate where handsome old buildings might be found, so I was obliged to conduct my own windshield survey. This unguided search failed to uncover many worthy examples, but I eventually collected 136 black-and-white photographs – enough to fill a hundred pages. These images comprised the first edition of *The Victorian Architecture of Iowa.*

The second photographic tour, conducted from 1994 to 1997, was more fruitful than the first. Hundreds of old buildings had by then been catalogued for the National Register of Historic Places, and two architectural historians – David Gebhard and Gerald Mansheim – had produced *Buildings of Iowa*, a guide book intended to be used exactly as I used it. My travels were also guided by the Iowan magazine, which in the intervening years had published a valuable series of articles on the architecture of particular towns.

Though this new collection of 248 photographs is more complete than the original, it still represents only a fraction of Iowa's 19th century architecture. Limited by the costs of publication, I chose to concentrate on domestic examples – homes and commercial buildings – at the expense of courthouses, schools, churches, and railroad stations. These omissions leave plenty of work for others to do, and I hope that future photo sleuths have as much fun as I did.

In the last twenty years a number of significant changes have occurred. Many of the examples in this collection were not included in the earlier edition because they were then in various states of disrepair. Since that time they have been made viewable again by an army of dedicated preservationists. In this respect there is actually more Victorian architecture now than there was before – at least there is more that demands to be photographed.

Another change concerns the use of color. In 1975 the choice of black-and-white film was appropriate because most buildings were covered with white paint, so that shapes and textures were the only things to see. As everyone who has traveled the state of Iowa will now attest, countless decorators have adopted semi-authentic "Painted Lady" color schemes, with striking results.

The final change worth noting is that one portion of the Victorian inventory has been greatly diminished by time. From 1880 on, millwork factories filled their catalogues with countless wooden pieces designed to beautify porches and rooflines. One could build a simple frame house of any shape, then apply a frosting of lathe-turned and jigsawed ornaments. Gable ends seem to have been popular longest, for they continued appearing in catalogues until at least 1915.

Because these wooden decorations could be easily added to just about anything, they could be as easily removed, and that's what has happened in the last twenty years. In 1975 I could drive down almost any rural road and expect to find an old farmhouse still equipped with decorative wooden elements. Now, however, they are rarely found. Some homeowners undoubtedly chose to modernize their houses by removing the unnecessary trappings of a bygone era. To that

These drawings were copied from photographs taken in 1975. Twenty years later the buildings remained, but the decorations were gone. Some gable ends, also called spandrels, could be adjusted to fit any slope. Others were designed specifically for 9:12, 10:12, and other popular roof pitches.

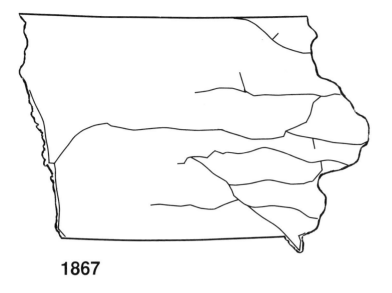
1867

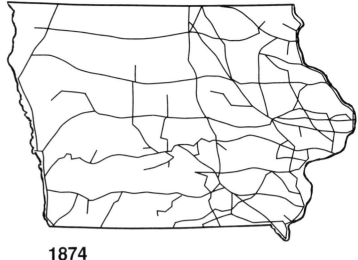
1874

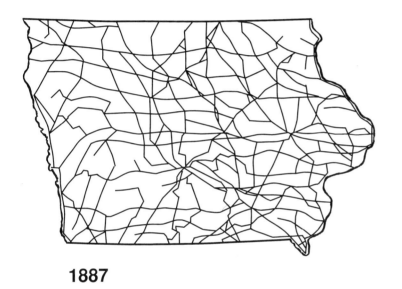
1887

Railroad Lines

The first railroads pushed straight across the open prairie, altering their routes only to match the contours of natural land forms. When the two great rivers had been joined, spur lines were laid to existing settlements. Wherever the tracks led, architecture followed.

cause, however, must be added the inexorable forces of wind and water that eventually take their toll on wooden structures.

In the final pages of the book the reader will find a map and location key. I tried to include examples from every part of the state, and from as many towns as possible, but the fact is that not all locations are equally endowed. Towns along the Mississippi River possess more examples because they were the first places settled and thus rose to prosperity at an earlier date. I have included three illustrations copied from railroad maps that help explain the resulting distribution. Builders often relied on manufactured components, so that the towns last reached by tracks were the last to acquire a measure of architecture.

Most of the buildings in this collection are found in Iowa's small cities and county-seat towns. Only a few are located in rural areas because 19th century farming was not sufficiently profitable to support stylized architecture. The few gentleman farmers who could afford to build handsome houses were exceptions to the rule. Rural prosperity was limited by low crop yields and low grain prices, and by the relatively small acreage that a family could work with horse-powered machinery. The merchants in the county-seat towns enjoyed a better cash flow, so that's where the most interesting buildings are found.

At the other end of the spectrum, Iowa's larger cities have less than their share of historic architecture. Many 19th century residential districts were gobbled up by expanding commercial cores. As the cities grew, Victorian mansions built to last a century were frequently knocked down after only 25 years. Older commercial buildings were similarly displaced.

Finally, I would like to offer a few comments about architectural scholarship. In 1975 there were very few books on the shelves to help researchers like me sort out the artistic history of the period. Most 20th-century authors thought that the Victorian era was a deplorably tasteless one whose products were of little interest and even less artistic merit. A typical commentary was penned in 1910 by architect Frank Wallis. He thought that the earlier work was "appalling" and would take "two or three generations more to live down." Lewis Mumford, a highly-regarded cultural critic, summed up the prevailing sentiment – the Victorian years were "The Brown Decades." Naturally, writers who disdained the Victorian repertoire were not eager to explain it.

Today's architectural historians take a different view, so information previously unavailable can now be found in periodical and hardcover literature. Surprisingly, however, no one has put all the pieces together. Most authors seem to feel that the reader's curiosity is limited to labels and distinguishing features, with the result that styles are identified but not explained. They will say, for example, that the Queen Anne label was created for "no very good reason." Having made that clear, they will refrain from saying what reason there may have been.

I have tried to assemble, from dozens of separate works, a coherent explanation of how architectural styles were created and disseminated. I hope that the little understanding I have gained may help others better appreciate the wonderfully diverse legacy of Victorian Architecture.

PHOTOGRAPHIC NOTE

Parallel lines – the corners of buildings – appear to converge if viewed from an angle other than 90 degrees. A large amount of convergence – looking up at a skyscraper – is generally acceptable because the human eye sees the same thing that the camera sees. Small amounts of convergence, however, are corrected in the perceptual process of seeing. We know that walls are perpendicular to the ground so we see them that way. The camera, however, has no such knowledge. When tilted up, it invariably turns rectangles into trapezoids.

Most of the photographs in this book were made with a Pentax 6x7cm camera (2.25 x 2.75 inch frame) equipped with a 75mm perspective correcting lens. The front element of the lens shifts off center, so that the camera can look up without tilting up. Smaller images were made with a Nikon F3 35mm camera fitted with a similar lens. Some closeup views were taken with the Pentax using a 200mm non-shift lens. In those cases, perspective adjustment was accomplished by skewing the images after they were scanned into Adobe Photoshop computer software. A few shots were retouched to eliminate evidence of peeling paint and other surface defects. All photographs were made on 120 Fuji Provia and 35mm Fuji Sensia transparency films with speeds of ASA 100.

William Plymat Jr.
Des Moines, Iowa
1997

1838

At four o'clock on the morning of June 28, 1838, the Queen was awakened by the sound of gunfire. It was not the beginning of an insurrection, merely an exuberant celebration of the status quo. Four hundred thousand British subjects were carousing in the streets of London. Bands played, voices were raised in song, and soldiers fired their muskets in the air. Before the day was over, a 19-year-old girl would be crowned Queen of England, the most powerful nation on Earth.

At daybreak the revelry subsided and all eyes were turned in the direction from which she would come. The young monarch stepped into a majestic coach and was driven slowly from Buckingham Palace to Westminster Abbey for an exhausting five-hour ceremony of religious devotion and secular homage. Having vowed to defend the empire, the Queen retreated to a private chamber to soak her hand in cold water. As she worked to remove the ring forced onto the wrong finger by the Archbishop, the multitude waited patiently.

After an hour's seclusion the Queen emerged to greet her subjects. The royal shoulders were draped in a robe of gold cloth lined with ermine. She carried the orb and scepter, and upon her head was seen the newly fashioned crown made from rubies, sapphires, and diamonds dating back to the 14th century. Trumpets sounded to cries of "God save the Queen." And God did. Victoria ruled for more than sixty years.

Styles of applied art had long been named for European monarchs, but it is especially fitting that American styles of the period are still called Victorian. The fact is, most of America's 19th century

Washington - Sunset Park on West Adams Street - 1840. Most early settlers lived in log cabins, though saw mills were among the first business establishments. Built by settler Alexandar Young on a farm north of town, this unusually large two-story cabin was moved and restored in 1912 by the Daughters of the American Revolution. Square-hewn logs are held together with V-notched corners. This type of construction was called Blockbau by the German immigrants who introduced it to Pennsylvania.

Iowa City - 604 Iowa Street - c. 1850. Federal Style brick houses were often built on limestone foundations.

Salem - 401 S. Main - c. 1840. The Lewelling House was built by an early Quaker settler who is thought to have harbored runaway slaves.

architecture was imported from England.

In 1838, Britain was at the height of her power. Undamaged by the Napoleonic Wars, she alone had the energy and resources to encircle the globe. It was the empire that surpassed Rome and upon which the sun never set. The War of Independence was still a vivid memory to many then living, yet American sensibilities were firmly rooted in British soil. If pioneers looked to the eastern seaboard for guidance in matters of taste, Easterners looked to England. Presidents came and went, but Victoria remained to give a lasting prefix to the attitudes and artifacts of the day.

There was, however, one class of Americans who would never be called Victorian. Their empire, equally old and steeped in tradition, was crumbling. Even in that early year they were a vanquished and dispossessed people, though the most famous battles were yet to be waged.

One leader of that people made camp during the summer of 1838 on the banks of the Des Moines River. He was Black Hawk, 70-year-old warrior chief of the Sac and Fox, tribes that had retreated from the Great Lakes through Wisconsin and Illinois to final defeat on the banks of the Mississippi.

In 1763 the Sac and Fox fought with Pontiac and the Ottawas in an unsuccessful attempt to halt white migration north of the Ohio River. They conquered 10 of the 14 frontier forts, only to be repulsed by succeeding waves of colonial soldiers. Pushed west, the Sac and Fox skirmished with the tribes of Illinois before settling in Iowa. This migratory history is not unique. Most of the tribes that populated Iowa in the 1830s – including the Winnebagos, Omahas, Missouris, and Pottawattamies – came from east of the great river. So what the United States bought from France in the Louisiana Purchase, it also bought from tribes who had been there only a short time. There were few battles, little bloodshed, but a great deal of paperwork.

In 1833, crushed by the brief war that bears his name, Black Hawk was taken to the nation's capital to meet the Great White Father. The chief's custodian was a young army officer who had staffed a frontier outpost in Iowa. Jefferson Davis would later win fame as President of the Confederacy.

It was common practice to discourage hostility by escorting native delegations to Washington. From the decks of steamboats the chiefs saw burgeoning towns and as many white faces as there were "blades of grass on the prairie." Most realized the futility of attempting to resist the onslaught of this vast migration. On meeting Andrew Jackson, a chastened Black Hawk said simply: "You are a man and I am another."

Having visited the seat of white government, the chief was returned to the agency camp east of Ottumwa. He spent the last few months of his life in a wigwam on the banks of the Des Moines River. It was made of posts set in the ground, covered with walnut bark and chinked with moss and mud. Black Hawk slept in a rawhide bunk on a dirt floor, a far cry from Buckingham Palace.

Taking his cue from the treaty of 1837, Old Hickory's successor presided over the creation of what would later become the 29th state. On June 12, 1838, President Martin Van Buren signed an act of Congress separating the lands west of the Mississippi from the Territory of Wisconsin. On July 4th, six days after the coronation of Victoria and three months before the death of Black Hawk, Iowa officially became a territory of the Union. In that year a census was taken. There were 22,589 settlers in Iowa, and virtually all spoke English.

The pioneers brought a few prized possessions from their former homes in

Riverdale - US 67 - c. 1844. This pioneer limestone house overlooking the Mississippi River was restored by ALCOA, which has a large plant on the other side of the highway.

Illinois, Indiana, Ohio, and Kentucky– the spinning wheel, the cast-iron stewpot, the muzzle-loading rifle, but most importantly, the axe. Disdaining the open prairies, early settlers built farms on bottom land in the forested strips that bordered the rivers. They chose these sites for the availability of building material, though they also labored under the mistaken notion that timbered soil was more fertile than the prairie.

Prior to 1838 the citizens of Iowa were squatters, unable to secure legal titles to the parcels they occupied. For protection they formed "claim clubs" to defend each other's property. When U.S. Land Offices opened in Dubuque and Burlington, 80-acre homesteads were auctioned at a starting price of $1.25 an acre. Anyone attempting to jump a claim by outbidding the squatter was a likely target of vigilante reprisal.

The log cabins built on these newly-registered homesteads were intended as temporary shelters. Within a few years the chores of planting and harvesting had become routine in the new land, the livestock was provided for, and the family had decided not to move farther west. It was then that the farmer traveled to a river town for millsawn lumber with which to build a proper house and barn.

In the years before the Civil War, countless wood-framed houses were built, though very few survive. They were chewed by termites and ravaged by the elements, and because all warmth and illumination was by flame, many simply burned. Those that remained were judged primitive by later standards and were replaced with more durable structures whenever family resources allowed. For these reasons, Iowa's oldest post-log structures are the ones built of stone and brick.

The predominant architectural style of the 1830s was the *Greek Revival,* but Iowa was still too young to fully partake of its luxury. Few were built, so Iowa now possesses only a handful of examples. Most were constructed after the tastemakers of the eastern cities had switched to other, equally derivative forms.

A more common type of architecture

Bentonsport - Front Street - 1846. Guests no longer arrive by steamboat, but at last report the Mason House continued to provide overnight accommodations. The hotel was built by Mormon laborers who, during their westward migration, stopped long enough to erect the sturdy brick walls.

Bentonsport - west edge of town - 1853. The James Brown house is one of the best examples of the Federal Style.

in the years before the Civil War was the *Federal Style*, or "the lingering Federal tradition" as it is sometimes characterized. These modestly proportioned homes lacked the rich decoration seen in the wealthy cities of Boston and Philadelphia. Most of Iowa's Federal houses are simple side-gabled boxes of brick or stone, owing more to the traditional shape of Colonial houses than to the classically-detailed estates of the eastern gentry.

Though the familiar Greek and Federal styles lasted through the 1850s, new fashions were evolving from antique sources. In June 1838, just as Iowa was getting its start, architect Alexander Jackson Davis arrived in Tarrytown, New York to supervise construction of a lavish home for William Paulding, a wealthy landowner. Lyndhurst, now managed as a museum by the National Trust for Historic Preservation, came to epitomize the *Gothic Revival*.

By 1829, Alexander Davis had distinguished himself as a talented architectural illustrator, and his drawings were published in popular magazines of the day. Entering the employ of Ithiel Town, a noted architect and engineer, the young Davis found himself in charge of the New York office when his patron unexpectedly sailed off on a European tour. Davis was soon designing in the obligatory Greek Revival idiom, and though his commissions were competently executed, they dissatisfied the young artist. Davis complained that it was becoming increasingly difficult to distinguish structural uses. Homes, banks, churches, and public buildings were all clothed in white-washed Doric columns.

The imaginative Davis was bored, so he deftly absorbed the latest European vogue. English architects were then

Oskaloosa - 2 miles northeast on Glendale Road - 1852-53. The Nelson Pioneer Farm has been part of a rural museum complex since 1964. The brick walls are 14 inches thick. The porch was added about 1900.

composing "essays in stone" to recreate the nostalgic flavor of medieval castles. Lyndhurst propelled Davis into the front rank of important American designers. In the early 1840s the prominent stylist made the acquaintance of a young man with a singular passion for picturesque settings. Beginning with a letter, then a meeting, Alexander Jackson Davis joined forces with Andrew Jackson Downing. By the end of the decade, a new American architecture had burst upon the scene.

Andrew - Highway 62 - 1852. Located about 14 miles from the Mississippi River, the Butterworth Inn was a stop on the stage line that ran from Davenport to Dubuque. The rectangular transom and side lights are associated with the Greek Revival, but the vernacular shape can best be categorized as Federal Survival.

Elkader - 101 High Street S.E. - 1850. This is a double-house – today we would call it a duplex – in the Greek Revival Style. There are nine rooms on each side.

The Federal Style — Old Forms for a New Land

The term *Federal Style* is used to classify American houses of the eastern seaboard built from about 1790 to 1830. Earlier Colonial forms were retained, but decorative treatments were influenced by Scottish architect Robert Adam.

Rooflines often featured tooth-like dentil blocks spaced along the cornice. Double-hung windows were symmetrically placed in brick walls and topped with flat stone lintels. High-fashion houses often displayed a Palladian Window – a tall circle-head sash flanked by smaller rectangular openings. Another exterior element unique to this period was a fanlight above the entry door.

Most of Iowa's early settlers adopted the typical form of late Colonial architecture – the side-gabled box. A gable is the angled portion of a wall formed by a roof that slopes in two directions. If the main entrance is in a gabled wall, the orientation is called "temple front." In Greek temples, the ends of the roof planes are connected with a protruding cornice and the resulting triangle is called a pediment. Americans seldom faced a gable toward the street until the advent of the Greek Revival.

Iowa was opened for settlement at about the time that the Federal Style is considered to have become obsolete, so "Federal Survival" is generally applied to any house built after 1840 that does not include Greek, Gothic, or Italianate forms. It is not clear who first used the term Federal Style, but it is unlikely that the builders of these Iowa houses associated them with any style at all.

Fort Madison - 421 Avenue E - c. 1850. This Federal Style home features a Classical entrance porch. The storm shutters are functional.

Council Bluffs - 231 Park Avenue - 1857. On Iowa's western frontier the Federal Style lingered longest.

Greek Revival   *Symbol of Democracy*

Ancient Roman elements, revived during the Italian Renaissance and exported to England in the 1600s, had been sparingly used in America since the 1740s. In 1762 a group of English archaeologists visited Athens and made measured drawings of the buildings on the Acropolis. Though it was obvious that the Italians had derived their columns from this older culture, Roman interpretations continued to supply the models for new designs in the *Classical Style.*

When he could spare the time, Thomas Jefferson added a columned portico to Monticello (1797-1809) and designed the Virginia state capitol to resemble the Roman temple he had seen at Nimes in France. Jefferson thought that the Classical forms perfectly expressed the new republic's civilized aspirations. Even so, very few houses of the Federal period employed free-standing columned porticos. Instead, rectangular pilasters were attached to walls to simulate the columned appearance.

Classical architecture gained impetus in 1821 when Greek patriots launched a war of independence against

Davenport - 224 E. 6th Street - 1856. By the time this house was constructed, the picturesque styles had largely supplanted the Greek Revival. The builder may have wanted to prove that he was not a slave to fashion.

the ruling Turks, a conflict for which Americans had great sympathy. The Doric, Ionic, and Corinthian orders were now seen to embody the principles of the Greek city states where democracy was born. Suddenly architecture discovered *associationalism,* the idea that the built environment could reflect political and spiritual values.

The popularity of the *Greek Revival* was so pervasive that Americans were soon calling it the "National Style." By 1840 enthusiasm had begun to wane, though the southern states never relinquished their love of white-washed columns and continued building in the Classical Style until the beginning of the Civil War.

The *Greek Revival* label is often applied to simple houses whose owners could not afford columns. Either a front-facing pedimented gable or a set of rectangular windows around the entry door is sufficient for inclusion in this style category. In Iowa in the 1840s, the lingering Federal form was more popular than the lingering Greek.

Muscatine - 205 Cherry Street - 1852. One can imagine steamboat passengers gazing up at this Greek Revival mansion. It is poised so close to the edge of a bluff that the only place from which to view it properly is the middle of the Mississippi River. The roof is topped with an octagon cupola.

1854

On February 22, 1854, the Chicago and Rock Island Railroad reached the banks of the Mississippi River. As soon as the last spike was driven, the construction firm of Sheffield and Farnam announced plans for a glorious excursion to celebrate the event. Dignitaries from eastern cities were invited to travel by train to Rock Island, there to embark on steamboats. They would ascend the Father of Waters to view the picturesque Falls of St. Anthony at a place later known as Minneapolis. The two great economic powers of the age – steamboats and steamtrains – would be harnessed to the same yoke. Nothing like it had ever been done.

The ascent of the Mississippi – "The Fashionable Tour" – had already attracted thousands of southern vacationers. To escape the summer heat of New Orleans and Memphis, ladies and gentlemen steamed north to Fort Snelling at the mouth of the Minnesota River. At the end of the gangplank, carriages waited to take the well-dressed gentry to a spot on the bluffs where they could view the falls. Sumptuous repasts were laid on blankets and, if musicians could be found, cotillions were danced on the prairie grass. There were mosquitos, of course, but the evening air was refreshingly cool.

In the early years, steamboat travel was a rustic affair as the boats then in service were primarily designed to carry freight. The first private staterooms are ascribed to the *Smelter,* a swift sidewheeler launched at Cincinnati in 1837. In 1838 the *Brazil* offered 30 staterooms fitted with berths, wash stands, and chamber pots. The first spring mattresses were installed on the *Malta* in 1839. When most of the boats were thus equipped, captains competed for fares with other touches of luxury. Soon brass ensembles and string quartets were entertaining the guests, and dining salons were laid with oriental carpets.

Despite a steady increase in passenger traffic, the greatest profits were earned by hauling ingots of lead down to St. Louis from the "mineral region." The mines at Dubuque continued to produce, but the largest cargos were loaded at the Illinois town of Galena, a short distance up the narrow Fever River. If they put on enough steam, some of the boats could log twenty round trips a year. A typical steamer made nine miles an hour upstream and almost fourteen on the way down, though the fastest boats did better.

William J. Petersen described this burgeoning trade in his 1937 book *Steamboating on the Upper Mississippi.* He told how Captain Harris left St. Louis in the Spring of 1845 and steered the *War Eagle* to Galena in the record time of 43 hours and 45 minutes.

Muscatine - 716 W. 3rd Street - c. 1851-56. The readoption of the cupola may have been suggested by the similarly tall, but more expensive, Italianate tower. The date of this house is uncertain, but has been traced to a five-year span.

"Some of the passengers on this trip expressed dissatisfaction with the treatment accorded them. Upon inquiry it was found that Captain Harris was considered too parsimonious with the meals, since only one dinner had been served on the trip. Further examination showed that the *War Eagle* had left St. Louis after dinner on Tuesday and had reached Galena before noon on Thursday. The disgruntled passengers were immediately informed that if they were traveling for dinners they would have to take a slower boat."

Vital to the operation of the boats were countless wood cutters who plied the banks of the river. Passing steamers were hailed and "wooding up" was conducted in haste. The licking flames of the huge boilers consumed vast quantities of native hardwood.

As the years passed, Iowa's river towns grew in population and soon could afford to charter steamboats for Sunday afternoon excursions. Merchants began the local subscription and school boys added their pennies to the purse for a

Muscatine - 606 W. 3rd Street - 1852. This is Iowa's best example of the early Italianate Style. The roof-mounted cupola, or belvedere, is exceptionally large, as are the carved wooden brackets. The brick walls are painted in muted tones that would have pleased A.J. Downing.

Bellevue - north edge of town - 1850. Records indicate that Mr. Wynkook purchased the land in 1848 and began his building campaign two years later. The result was an impressive limestone dwelling with finials topping the bargeboards. Square towers were part of the original Gothic repertoire, but were seldom included in America's Gothic designs. Given the simultaneous evolution of the towered Italianate, one supposes that the designer of this house chose to combine the two styles. It is now a bed-and-breakfast inn.

chance to stand at the rail. The boats were draped with banners, flags, and flowers, and filled with as many town residents as could squeeze aboard.

They set out from Dubuque, Clinton, Davenport, Muscatine, Burlington, Ft. Madison, and Keokuk. In hopes of winning paragraphs of praise from newspaper editors, the captains spared no effort or expense. They might race downstream under a full head of steam to give everyone a thrill, then churn slowly back to the landing at twilight.

By the time of the Great Excursion of 1854, the pathways of the great river had been well charted and boat captains had rehearsed their acts. The inland farmer might huddle in his log cabin and worry about what the chinch bugs were doing to his wheat, but the river folk could afford a more carefree demeanor. They shared a piece of civilization.

So it was that on the morning of June 5, 1854, the collected dignitaries assembled at Chicago's Rock Island station. There were politicians, businessmen, clergymen and professors, but most importantly, newspaper writers. Stepping aboard two nine-coach trains were scribblers from the Boston *Atlas,* Albany *Evening Journal,* New York *Tribune,* and Cincinnati *Gazette,* to name only a few.

After a stop for lunch the trains arrived in Rock Island at four o'clock and began loading passengers onto five steamboats. These were quickly filled, so two additional boats were added to the armada. When the final accommodations proved inadequate, many of the less important guests were returned, boatless, to Chicago. In all, 1,200 passengers were taken aboard, though some were obliged to sleep on pallets strewn about the dining floors.

Captain Harris in the *War Eagle* was first to cast off. The *Golden Era,* carrying former President Millard Fillmore, brought up the rear, and all were underway by ten o'clock that night. Watching the boats depart were countless hundreds of other travelers who were preparing to take their rest on the banks of the river. In a newspaper item that year, the *Rock Islander* reported:

"Hundreds of muslin-covered wagons, bearing wives and children, and household goods, and driven by stalwart men, seeking a new home in the mighty West, cross the Mississippi at this point weekly. It is a tide which knows no ebb."

The *Davenport Commercial* saw the same sight from the opposite shore.

"Our ferry is busy all hours in passing over the large canvas-backed wagons, densely populated with becoming Iowaians. An army of mechanics have added 300 buildings to this city during the past season, yet every nook and corner of them are engaged before they are finished... There is not a vacant dwelling or business room in the city."

At Burlington the steam ferry was kept constantly in motion, often till midnight, yet still the Illinois bank was crowded with impatient immigrants. The *Telegraph* reported that wagons were deposited in Iowa at the rate of six or seven hundred a day. The *Dubuque Reporter* noted:

"Viewing the almost countless throng of immigrants that crowd our streets, and learning that a similar scene is visible at every other point along the Mississippi border of Iowa, the spectator is naturally led to infer that a general exodus is taking place in the Eastern States of the Union… Day by day the endless procession moves on – a mighty army of invasion."

Inland towns also saw the coming and going of this wandering tribe. The *Oskaloosa Times* noted that the roads were thronged with covered wagons trailing herds of cattle. The passing population was estimated at a thousand a week.

Though these news items were copied by the eastern papers, the Great Expedition of 1854 garnered the largest headlines. In the days that followed their departure the boats made port at all the major towns and splendid speeches were delivered. At times the boats were lashed together so that the travelers could exchange pleasantries. Fond reacquaintances were accomplished by young men who, after the train ride, had been separated from certain young ladies.

A writer for the New Haven

Burlington - 303 S. 6th Street - c. 1852. The year 1852 seems to mark the beginning of the cupolaed Italianate Style in Iowa. The window caps are made of cast iron.

Mount Pleasant - 401 N. Main Street - 1858. An octagon cupola tops the tallest wing of this bracketed villa. The front porch was enlarged about 1925, but the classical columns are thought to be original.

Wynkook house is Iowa's premier example of the *Bargeboard Style*.

The stalwart steamboats that once paddled past the Bellevue bluffs have long since disappeared. Some sank, some burned, most were cut up for scrap. Floating architecture, sad to say, cannot long survive. The only architecture that can last from 1854 to the present day is the architecture rooted in soil, though even that takes an extraordinary bit of luck. Thousands of houses were built along the river in the years before the Civil War, but only a few survive. The historic architecture left to enjoy is a tiny sprig of the original forest.

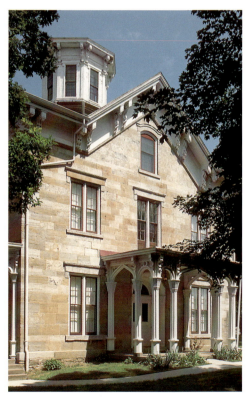

Dubuque - 2241 Lincoln Avenue - 1857. The Ham House, now the central fixture of a northside park, was fashioned from well-cut limestone blocks.

Palladium described the meals aboard his boat:

"We have had oysters and lobsters daily, though two thousand miles from the sea. These, of course, were brought in sealed cans. Hens, turkeys, and ducks have given their last squeak every morning. Two cows on the lower deck furnish us with fresh milk twice a day."

Passing Bellevue on the west bank, excursionists pointed to a handsome house on a bench of land set back from the river. This home, belonging to Mr. Wynkook, was a newly minted example of *Gothic Revival* architecture. "Just like back east," they must have said, for in the valley of that other great river, the Hudson, such houses were plentiful. Surely Mr. Wynkook's house had been copied from a page of Mr. Downing's book.

Actually, no. Mr. Downing did not publish the design of Mr. Wynkook's house, though some other author of architectural patterns must have. The

Davis & Downing   *The Picturesque Movement*

Alexander Jackson Davis (1803-1892) inked the drawings while Andrew Jackson Downing (1815-1852) crafted the words. Though the similarity of names caused some confusion, the two men were of notably different stripes. Davis was a methodical craftsman. Downing was a zealous promoter.

Andrew Downing sold nursery stock to the prosperous landowners of the Hudson River valley. In 1841, at the age of 26, he penned *A Treatise on the Theory and Practice of Landscape Gardening, Adapted to North America*. Expanding his interests to include architecture, Downing published *Cottage Residences* in 1842 and *The Architecture of Country Houses* in 1850. The last of these went through nine editions and 16,000 copies before the end of the Civil War. The books owed their commercial success to the detailed engravings of Alexander Davis. The two groundbreakers were now fully absorbed in what has been called the *Picturesque Movement*.

The 18th century Age of Enlightenment fostered a new set of artistic values. The beauties of nature were extolled by artists and poets who saw in their surroundings the roots of a spiritual awakening. Beauty in any form was ennobling. The stage was thus set for *Romanticism*, the artistic mood that prevailed in Europe and America in the first half of the 19th century.

The Romantics had an affinity for untamed nature and atmospheric settings. Painters of the day delighted in crafting mystical scenes filled with picturesque villas and tumbled down Gothic ruins enveloped in ethereal light. These nostalgic ideals found their way naturally from the fine art of canvas to the practical art of carpentry.

By 1830, Gothic literature was also a cultural fixture. In 1764, Horace Walpole, son of a British prime minister, published *The Castle of Otranto,* the first Gothic novel. Walpole's Strawberry Hill near London was originally a small

Keokuk - 507 N. 4th Street - 1855. The Italian Villa popularized by Davis and Downing called for a square tower, not a cupola.

Washington - 504 W. Washington Street - late 1850s. Though the slope is wrong, the designer may have been trying to execute a Mansard roof. The window openings are Italianate and the miniature bargeboard cusps are Gothic.

country house, but in 1749 the eccentric author began remodeling it to resemble a medieval castle. He wrote of the "satisfaction of imprinting the gloomth of the abbeys and cathedrals on one's house."

Between 1812 and 1819 the famous poet Sir Walter Scott built a Gothic castle called Abbotsford in the Scottish highlands. There he penned many of his Gothic novels, including *Rob Roy*, *Ivanhoe*, and *The Bride of Lammermoor* – tales in which chivalrous knights performed feats of valor. After Scott's death in 1832 his castle attracted pilgrims from all over the English-speaking world. Having visited Scotland in 1834, James Fenimore Cooper, author of the *Last of the Mohicans* and other buckskin fables, went back to New York and promptly built a Gothic castle of his own.

The first Gothic composition by Alexander Davis was Glenellen, a country house near Baltimore built in 1832. In 1837 he published *Rural Residences*, the first American pattern book to show scaled drawings of complete houses. Earlier builders' guides offered technical advice and views of ornamental Greek elements, but Davis was the first to categorize the shapes of buildings and provide detailed floor plans. He had the merchandise, but he needed Downing's help to capture the emerging market.

Andrew Downing thought that a home in the city, fitted snugly to a narrow lot, might appropriately present a stern Federalist face to the passing world. A country home, on the other hand, should be expansive, rambling, and robust – a domestic adornment wrapped in nature's sweeping vista. In 1850 he wrote:

"What an unfailing barrier against vice, immorality, and bad habits, are those tastes which lead us to embellish a home, to which at all times and in all places we turn with delight, as being the object and the scene of our fondest cares, labors, and enjoyments; whose humble roof, whose shady porch, whose verdant lawn and smiling flowers, all breathe forth to us, in true, earnest tones, a domestic feeling that at once purifies the heart, and binds us more closely to our fellow beings!"

To Downing, a man's home really was his castle, Gothic or otherwise, and it could be otherwise. In the romantic vocabulary of the Picturesque Movement, there were two kinds of houses – cottages and villas – and two styles in which they could be decorated – Gothic and Classic.

In 1852, as Gothic cottages and Classical villas were being erected throughout the land, 37-year-old A.J. Downing left his own Gothic home in the picturesque Hudson valley and bought passage on a steamboat bound for New York City. He soon learned that the captain of his vessel had arranged to race another boat. The boilers overheated, the boat caught fire, and Downing's body was later found floating in shallow water. He was a strong swimmer, it was said, and could not have drowned. Some had seen him on the hurricane deck, moments before the flames engulfed him. He could have saved himself, they said, but instead spent his last moments flinging chairs into the water to help keep others afloat.

In this regard as well, A.J. Davis was of a different stripe. He lived the last 32 of his 89 years in prosperous retirement.

Burlington - 607 N. 5th Street - 1858. The highly symmetrical Tuscan Villa is one branch of the Italianate family tree.

Gothic Revival *Romantic Medieval Sentiments*

When Augustus Welby Northmore Pugin (1812-1852) married his third wife, the first two having died, he proclaimed: "A first-rate Gothic woman at last, who perfectly understands and delights in spires and chancels." It must have taken a sturdy Gothic spirit indeed to share a Gothic roof with the easily perturbed Mr. Pugin, a man regarded even by his friends as a disputatious reactionary. Before his short life was finished, the former theatrical set painter had designed almost a hundred English churches. With all that going on, he still found time to scribble, so his lasting fame was churned from the bookseller's presses.

Pugin found the Classical motifs entirely galling. A devout Catholic, he noted that the Greeks and Romans were heathens, so their columns, entabulatures, and pediments were godless. Good Christian Gothic was England's only proper style, and he was delighted to help Sir Charles Barry give the new

Keokuk - 710 N. 7th Street - 1856.
A steep bargeboard shelters a recessed window that features a four-lobed element known as a quatrefoil. The flanking chimneys draw their shapes from the Tudor period.

Decorah - 503 West Broadway - 1861 or 1862. The spindled porch was probably added in the 1880s, but did little to alter the effect of the original Gothic composition.

houses of Parliament a respectable Gothic costume. When not thumping the Classicists, the otherwise single-minded Pugin enjoyed sailing his yacht off the rocky coast of England.

The Gothic cathedrals of Europe were constructed over a period of four hundred years beginning about 1140, but the evolving style was never called Gothic by its inventors. The word was a derogatory term coined by Italian artists of the 15th century. Because the Goths had sacked Rome in 476, anything barbarous and undignified was Gothic. By the time 19th century historians got around to unraveling the mysteries of the flying buttress, the origin of the term had been all but forgotten.

American castles like Glenellen and Lyndhurst were fine for those who could afford them, but the working class needed a more accessible kind of Gothic. By 1839, Pugin had published a collection of 30 bargeboards from 16th century manor houses. This folio, with large engravings suitable for copying, was promptly imported by American designers.

The bargeboard, also known as a vergeboard, was a somewhat practical but largely decorative medieval feature. Fashioned from a plank of lumber and running the full length of a gabled roofline, the bargeboard helped shelter plaster walls from the elements. More importantly, its foliated scroll work was the principal ornamental feature of the timber-frame manor house.

It is remarkable that a single design element can define a genre, but such was the case with the new *Gothic Revival*. The repertoire included pointed-arch windows with diamond pane glazing, bay windows, vertical board-and-batten siding, and assorted ornamental devices like finials, crockets, and roof crestings. However, a perfectly Gothic house might have square window openings, no bay windows, and no ornamental devices. The important thing was that it had bargeboards and looked picturesque.

The term *Carpenter Gothic* is often used to differentiate vernacular wood-frame houses from academic stone castles like Lyndhurst. Untutored carpenters, pattern books in hand, played the role of architect and brought the first touch of style to the recently settled frontier.

Italianate *Classical Ideals in Picturesque Clothes*

Classical architecture had enjoyed a long run of popularity dating back to Inigo Jones and Christopher Wren, the great English architects of the 17th century. For the first 150 years the Classical influence was largely decorative. The shapes of houses continued to follow traditional forms until the last manifestation – the Greek Revival – finally popularized the fully-columned facade.

With the Greek style waning, architects reinvented the Classical by scooping another bucket of precedent from the deep well of the Italian Renaissance. The first Italian examples appeared in England soon after 1800, and American versions were popular by 1845.

Historians have subdivided the Italian genre into a number of categories. Davis and Downing promoted the *Italian Villa* – a rambling, asymmetrical pile with roofs of various heights around a tall square tower. Queen Victoria's consort, Prince Albert, gave this style a boost by collaborating with Thomas Cubitt on the design of Osborne House, a royal retreat on the Isle of Wight. Built from 1845 to 1851, the gracious estate featured a pair of Italian towers that, because they were unwindowed, were called campaniles.

Many of the Italian prototypes had been expanded over the centuries so that verandas and wings sprawled out from the main structure in several directions. This varied appearance was pleasing to advocates of the picturesque, and the expansiveness of the format offered unrivaled design flexibility. Downing wrote:

"A villa, however small, in the Italian style, may have an elegant and expressive character, without interfering with convenient internal arrangement, while at the same time, this style has the very great merit of allowing additions to be made in almost any direction, without injuring the effect of the original structure."

By comparison, the *Tuscan Villa* was a model of decorum. Imported from the rocky northern province of Tuscany, it relied on cubical symmetry and formal composition. In America the elements of the two villa styles were seldom differentiated, so that the Italian and Tuscan labels were often used interchangeably.

The *Palladian Style*, named for 16th century architect Andrea Palladio, was more closely related to the original Roman temples. Features included a centered entrance portico and pedimented roof projection, usually tied to a pavilion pushed out a few feet from the main body of the building.

Davenport - 510 W. 6th Street - 1857. Perched high on a hill overlooking the downtown business district, this towered Italian Villa is a rare specimen. Though somewhat disfigured by inappropriate additions, the roofline retains the original decor. When photographed, it was in the process of receiving a multi-colored paint scheme.

21

Manchester - 120 Union Street E. - 1864. The cupola, or belvedere, began its long career in 17th century England.

The wooden bracket is the unifying element of the Italianate family.

Visually distinct, but sharing many of the same principles, was the *Pallazo Style*, more often called *Renaissance Revival*. This urban block was defined by overhanging roof cornices and rows of projected window moldings. Subtract the academic details and you had the *Italianate* house, a square box with a cupola in the center of a shallow pyramidal roof. There was also an Italianate townhouse with a sidehall entrance and windows topped with decorative caps.

In practice it is often difficult to say exactly which of these hats a particular house is wearing. If the composition is too eclectic to sort out, just call it *Hudson River Bracketed* after a novel of that title by 19th century writer Edith Wharton.

The rooftop cupola is the most striking design element of the Italianate family. Also known as a belvedere, lantern, or observatory, the cupola was a relatively small windowed room at the top of a house whose only real purpose was to facilitate ventilation. Letting summer heat escape through the roof helped bring cool air in through lower windows.

In Iowa and other midwestern states, towered villas were rare but cupolas were plentiful, a fact that has never been satisfactorily explained. For that matter, the origin of the cupola itself is surprisingly obscure. By failing to distinguish its source, contemporary style books leave readers with the erroneous idea that it must be Italian.

In his book *Early American Architecture*, Hugh Morrison explained that the cupola was invented in the mid 17th century by unknown English builders. Indeed, something rather like a cupola does show up on English examples of that date, and on a few American houses of the Colonial period. It was usually a small hexagonal structure protruding from the roof of a gabled house. George Washington put one on the roof of Mount Vernon, and small boxy cupolas appeared on a few Federal and Greek houses of the 1820s and 30s. So how did the cupola become such a prominent feature of the new Italian mode? The assumption is that it resembled the similarly tall, but more expensive, Italian tower.

One likely candidate for cupola-revival credit is Philadelphia architect Samuel Sloan who published *The Model Architect* in 1852. The date of that work coincides with Iowa's earliest cupolaed houses in Burlington and Muscatine. The question is, did Sloan propagate the idea, or did all the designers fall in love with cupolas at precisely the same moment?

Cupolas seem so odd to contemporary observers that extraordinary efforts have been made to shroud them in myth and fable. Whenever a cupola is encountered, still alive and well after all these years, there is usually a quaint anecdote to go with it. The owner, it is said, spent hours there, peering through narrow windows for some eccentric purpose, such as the surveillance of workmen in nearby factory yards, or the counting of steamboats on the river. Most unlikely of all is the notion that these high windowed rooms were used to spot marauding Indians. The real reason for the building of cupolas was that everyone else was building them.

The unifying element of the Italianate category is the bracket, an L-shaped piece of carved wood tucked up under the eaves. The Renaissance prototypes–known as consoles and modillions–featured foliated Classical designs, but American varieties displayed a wide range of indigenous shapes. Some builders, fearful of appearing too ostentatious, kept their brackets simple, with a minimal display of the woodcarver's art, while others welcomed the richest of ornamentation. Long after cupolas had disappeared, the decorative bracket remained in vogue.

Waterloo - 520 W. 3rd Street - 1861. The Russell House is now owned by a community association. The Italianate design features a columned veranda.

Grinnell - 927 High Street - c. 1870s. Multi-colored paint schemes serve to highlight the decorative details.

Decorah - 509 W. Broadway - 1860. Though the columned entrance porch is associated with the early years of the Italianate Style, it appears to be a holdover from the Greek Revival. Both styles were Classically derived.

Octagon *Governing Form of Nature*

Muscatine - Hwys 61 and 38 - 1855. Most Octagons employed the Italianate vocabulary, but this example is surprisingly plain. The small gables in the brick cupola are very unusual.

The *Octagon Mode* was the brainchild of Orson Squire Fowler, a phrenologist and public speaker. His book *A Home For All – The Gravel Wall and Octagon Mode of Building* was published in 1848 and appeared in six editions in the following eight years. The author built his own octagon at Fishkill, New York with walls of concrete, his favorite building material. If was four stories tall and boasted 65 rooms.

Though polygonal buildings had existed for centuries, Fowler publicized the fact that an octagon yields one-fifth more floor space than a rectangle of equal perimeter. He wrote: "What a vast number of steps will the octagon save a large and stirring family over the square." Fowler maintained that heating and ventilation were facilitated by his novel floor plans, but the real charm was that the octagon approached the sphere – "the predominant and governing form of Nature."

One authority estimates that Iowa originally had 38 octagon houses. Only a few survive.

Dubuque - 1095 3rd Street W. - 1857. The Langworthy house is the finest of Iowa's remaining Octagons. Architect John F. Rague also designed the Old Capitol in Iowa City.

Newton - 322 N. 8th Avenue E. - c. 1865. The first cylindrical towers were built during the Romanesque period of European history, but continued to appear on castles built during the Gothic centuries. This is Iowa's oldest example.

Vinton - 1003 B Avenue - 1867. At the beginning of the 20th century, cupolas were routinely removed from countless Italianate houses. Happily, this one escaped modernization. Paint scrapings confirm that the original colors were similar to those now in use.

1865

On April 1, 1865, General Robert E. Lee sent a message to Jefferson Davis, President of the Confederacy.

"The movement of General Grant to Dinwiddie Court House seriously threatens our position, and diminishes our ability to maintain our present lines in front of Richmond and Petersburg."

While the telegrapher was tapping out this urgent dispatch, General George Pickett was placing his remaining infantry along the White Oak Road. Confidently, he set them to building breastworks.

As the Confederates felled trees and piled the logs chest high, they sensed no anxiety in their leader. There would be no charge this day – nothing like the fateful rush up Cemetery Ridge at Gettysburg where three-quarters of Pickett's men were slaughtered. After the previous day's engagements, they thought, the worst to be expected was a glancing blow from Phil Sheridan's cavalry. They could not know that Sheridan was preparing to throw 12,000 infantry against them. The climactic battle of the Civil War was about to unfold.

Satisfied with his military disposition, General Pickett withdrew from the line to take dinner with General Thomas Rosser who had just ridden in from the Shenandoah Valley to bolster the sagging Confederate lines. As the officers dined on shadfish roasted over coals, a courier brought word that the enemy was advancing in unexpected numbers. Just then a line of bluecoats emerged from the woods and opened fire. The rebel commanders were cut off from their troops.

Meanwhile, a half continent away, a snug little steamboat was churning its way up the Missouri River with a cargo of goods consigned to the Fort Benton

Cedar Falls - 603 Clay Street - 1866. An architect who liked both prevailing styles might decide to squeeze them together. In this case, however, the Italianate window caps are made of stamped-metal rather than cast iron, which suggests that they may have been installed some time after the Gothic bargeboards.

gold camps. The *Bertrand*, launched the previous November at Wheeling, West Virginia, had made her way down the Ohio River to St. Louis. How she became enrolled in the mountain trade is uncertain, but the demand for boats was high and no fewer than eight vessels were ready to steam for the gold fields in March when the Missouri's waters reached a navigable depth.

The Bertrand measured 161 feet, had a stated capacity of 251 tons, and drew 18 inches of water. In advance of her departure a St. Louis newspaper boomed her chances. Passengers seeking transportation to Fort Benton, Virginia City, Deer Lodge, and the Bitter Root Valley could not do better. Said the paper: "Shippers may rely on this being one of the first boats to Benton."

Well prepared though she was, the Bertrand's passage was not without hazards. At Omaha travelers could disembark and spend a comfortable night at the Herndon House, a handsome brick hotel. But from that point on, river conditions were treacherous and the passing terrain increasingly desolate. Above Sioux City, the last outpost of civilization, the course ran alternately north and west through South Dakota, North Dakota, then two-thirds of Montana, a total distance of more than two thousand miles.

Stuffed into the little steamer's five-foot hold was an amazing assortment of civilized goods. Under the heading of tinned and bottled foodstuffs, the alphabetical listing began with ale and almonds and moved on to bitters

ample supply of tobacco on board. Yet it was all barely enough to satisfy the gold-whetted appetites of hard-wintered prospectors. No distant war could lure these rough men from the claims they had squatted on since 1862.

As the Bertrand was swinging round a bend in the Missouri River about 25 miles north of Council Bluffs, soldiers in far off Virginia were embroiled in the Battle of Five Forks. Rebel artillery roared double cannister shot into the ranks of staggering bluecoats, but still the enemy surged forward.

Just then, at about one o'clock in the afternoon, Missouri River time, the Bertrand plowed into a hidden snag,

Decorah - 301 Upper Broadway - 1867. Ornate bargeboards were removed in the 1930s, but this house still retains its picturesque Gothic flavor.

Des Moines - Hickman Road at I-35/80 - 1867. The Flynn Mansion is the architectural centerpiece of Living History Farm, a museum dedicated to Iowa's pioneer heritage. Restoration of the Italianate house required rebuilding the missing chimneys and stripping white paint from brick walls.

and bourbon, then candy, catsup, and cherries. Groceries included hazelnuts, honey, and horseradish, pickles, pineapples, and prunes.

In the category of textiles and wearing apparel, one could find everything from belts and blankets to pins and plackets, slickers and socks, ties and trousers. The alphabet of household items commenced with almanacs, brooms, and candles, proceeded to goblets and griddles, encompassed waffle irons and washboards, and ended with, what else, whiskey glasses.

There was plenty of hardware in the hold. Anvils and auger bits, levels and lock assemblies, screws and screw drivers, sleigh bells and spoke shaves, tar paper and thumb latches. Even window frames. Last, but not least, there was an

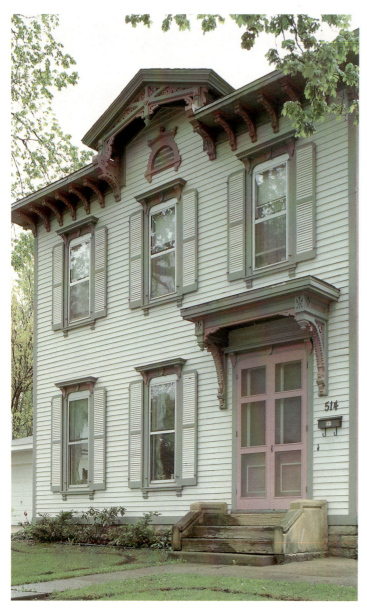

Boone - 514 Carroll Street - 1865. A few blocks from where his track gangs were drinking their pay in crude frame saloons, John Insley Blair, president of the Cedar Rapids and Missouri Railroad, built a proper Italianate house. He sold it in 1868.

Council Bluffs - 605 S. 3rd Street - 1869. This famous home, now a museum, was built for Grenville Dodge, a noted Civil War general who, at the time of construction, was chief engineer for the Union Pacific Railroad. The Classical entrance porch was added in 1907.

ripped a hole in her hull, and sank in five minutes, immersing in shallow water a cargo valued at more than $100,000. The cabin deck was awash, but the pilot house was dry. Women and children were deposited on the river bank as men hurriedly began taking off whatever could be quickly salvaged. Crates were stacked to provide a temporary shelter, though most of the passengers found overnight lodging in homes at nearby Desoto Bend.

After nightfall, word of the battle reached General Grant's headquarters. The Union commander sat before a blazing fire, a cigar in his mouth. The courier, Horace Porter, wrote:

"I began shouting the good news as soon as I got in sight and in a moment all but the imperturbable commander-in-chief were on their feet giving vent to wild demonstrations of joy…grasping of hands, tossing up hats, slapping backs."

After four years of horror, victory was at hand. In a few days it would all be over. Abe Lincoln would lie in state, felled by an assassin's bullet, but at least Iowa's men would be coming home.

Iowa sent more than 72,000 troops to fight on the distant battlefields of the Civil War – nearly half the men of military age. Of those who volunteered, 13,000 never returned and 8,500 were wounded. Seven thousand Iowans fought at the Battle of Shiloh in southern Tennessee. Others died at Vicksburg, Chattanooga, and Lookout Mountain.

Mt. Pleasant - 405 N. Broadway - 1868. This handsome specimen is thoroughly Italian. There's an imposing tower, a set-back wing of lower elevation, and a columned veranda. Finishing touches include paired eave brackets and round-topped windows with projecting caps. For most of its life – at least as far back as 1891 – the brick walls were painted in a variety of colors.

By September 1864, General Sherman had captured Atlanta. Of the 31,000 casualties reported in that action, 2,500 were Iowans.

The history books lead one to believe that apart from the war, nothing much was going on. Quite the contrary. The Civil War did less to slow private-sector economic activity than the financial crash of 1857.

The construction of a railroad from Clinton to Council Bluffs began in 1853, but it took the rest of the decade to reach Cedar Rapids and the first two construction companies went bust. In 1860 a new line, the Cedar Rapids and Missouri Railroad, was organized by John Insley Blair of New Jersey. Despite the shortage of labor, Blair managed to field track gangs throughout the war. The rails reached Marshalltown in 1862, and in 1864 the line threw a bridge across the river at Clinton so that passengers could forgo the accustomed ferry ride.

In 1865 the end of track was at the temporary town of Montana, 200 miles west of the Mississippi. It was not much of a town – a couple hundred frame buildings thrown together on a stretch of open prairie without a tree in sight. The single street, sixty feet wide, was full of rough looking men with wide-brimmed hats and pants in their boots, armed and looking for trouble. Stage coaches left daily for Council Bluffs, and one who was about to move on was G. Smith

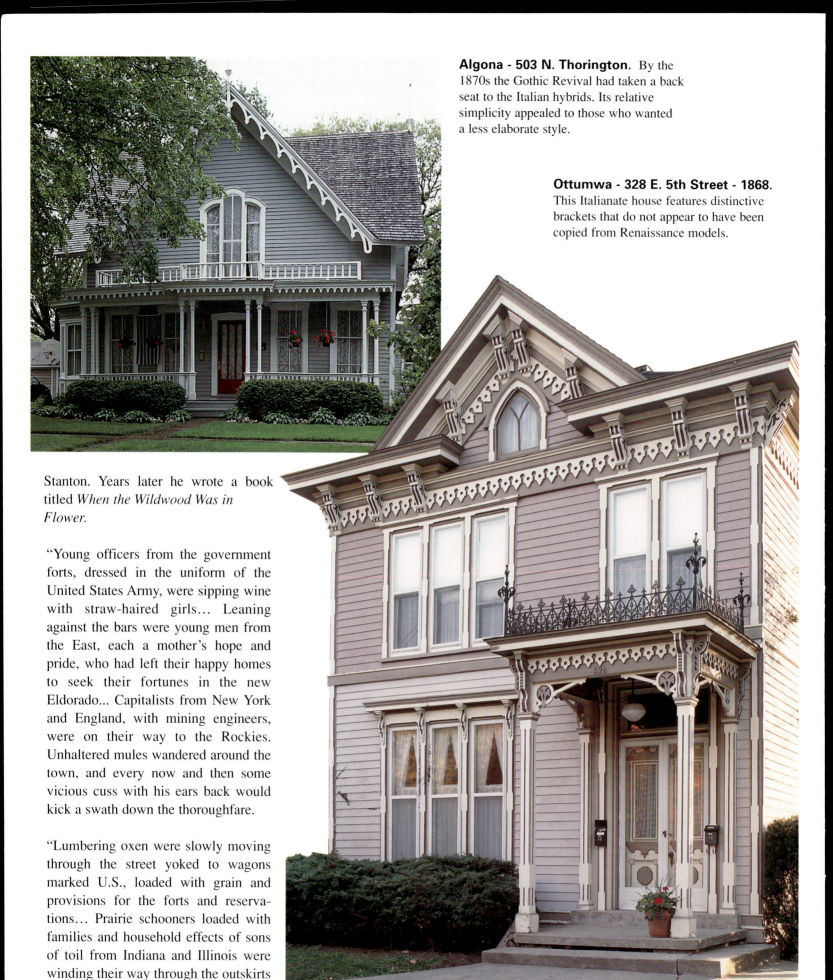

Algona - 503 N. Thorington. By the 1870s the Gothic Revival had taken a back seat to the Italian hybrids. Its relative simplicity appealed to those who wanted a less elaborate style.

Ottumwa - 328 E. 5th Street - 1868. This Italianate house features distinctive brackets that do not appear to have been copied from Renaissance models.

Stanton. Years later he wrote a book titled *When the Wildwood Was in Flower.*

"Young officers from the government forts, dressed in the uniform of the United States Army, were sipping wine with straw-haired girls… Leaning against the bars were young men from the East, each a mother's hope and pride, who had left their happy homes to seek their fortunes in the new Eldorado... Capitalists from New York and England, with mining engineers, were on their way to the Rockies. Unhaltered mules wandered around the town, and every now and then some vicious cuss with his ears back would kick a swath down the thoroughfare.

"Lumbering oxen were slowly moving through the street yoked to wagons marked U.S., loaded with grain and provisions for the forts and reservations… Prairie schooners loaded with families and household effects of sons of toil from Indiana and Illinois were winding their way through the outskirts of the town to accept Uncle Sam's hospitality and settle on the great plains

Keokuk - 202 Blondeau - early 1860s. Built sometime during the Civil War – the exact date is uncertain – this house is an early example of the new Second Empire Style.

Centerville - Valley Drive - c. 1870. A small, ornamented entrance porch was a common Italianate feature.

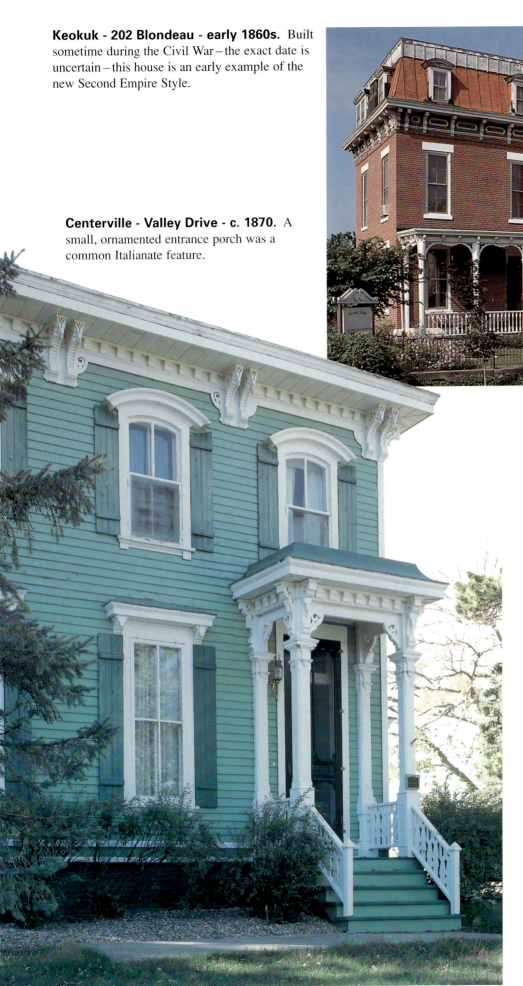

beyond. Herds of grass-fed cattle, smooth and fat, were arriving from the luscious grasses of the Missouri River plateau to be shipped to the Eastern markets, and paid-off cowboys would ride on bucking ponies through the dance houses shooting daylight through the roofs."

When the road gangs moved on, the town of Montana relaxed, settled down, and was renamed Boone.

Abe Lincoln knew it was important to continue building. Throughout the long war he kept crews working to complete the unfinished dome of the nation's capitol. Built in the 1820s, the first dome was a puny affair made of wood. Reconstruction began in 1855 with an iron framework of more suitable proportions. Lincoln took his 1861 inaugural oath in the shadow of this imposing but unfinished structure. In a sense, the capitol dome was a symbol of the nation's fate. The cementing of the union and the cementing of the nation's architectural stones were inevitably locked in time.

So the battlefields of the great war were not the only venues of human endeavor. The nation had energy and

Decorah - 401 West Broadway - 1867. This Italian Villa gained a Queen Anne porch sometime before 1900. From 1904 to 1968 the home belonged to Adelbert Field Porter, who built rock and mineral specimens into the wall fronting the grounds. It now belongs to the Winneshiek County Historical Society.

money to invest in other things, as the voyage of the Bertrand amply demonstrated. The important thing about the Bertrand is not that she set out to haul exotic freight to far-off gold diggers. The more significant cargo is the one she carried on her maiden voyage. Filling the hold on that inaugural trip down the Ohio River from Wheeling were 6,000 kegs of nails.

Houses were then built on the balloon-frame system, a structural technique made possible by manufactured nails. Before 1800, nails were expensive. A smithy would pull a strip of hot iron from a forge and hammer slivers into the desired shape. By 1807 machines had been made that could cut a roll of wire into precise lengths, incise a sharp point on one end, and affix a head to the other. At 25 cents a pound the first mass-produced nails were still too costly, but by 1833 the price had dropped to five cents a pound. Houses no longer had to be made from thick posts and beams, nor held together with mortise and tenon joints. A hastily-assembled basketwork of 2x4s would do the trick. That and plenty of cheap nails.

By 1865 the "Battle of the Styles" had been waged in England for at least thirty years. Instead of arguing about which architecture was most visually appealing, backers of the two great styles attacked each other on ethical

Pella - 4 miles south on 163 - 1871. The Mansard roof displays the date of construction in colored slate shingles. Distinctive features include large Italianate brackets and oval attic windows.

Des Moines - 644 9th Street - 1873.
Before the era of "urban renewal," the hill north of Des Moines' business district was covered with handsome houses, but this is the only survivor. The decorated entrance and cast window caps are wonderfully Italianate.

grounds. Classicists said the Gothic was mordant, Gothicists said the Classic was impure. Every architect loved one style and hated the other. When the victories were counted, the Battle of the Styles ended with a clear winner.

The waning of Gothic's popularity has been ascribed to a variety of associational difficulties. From the outset, Gothic seemed stuffy and superstitious, while the buoyant Italianate was fresh and dignified. A God-fearing man might prefer to worship in a Gothic sanctuary with a proper Gothic steeple overhead, but he really did not savor the idea of living in a church. One architect wrote that clients were "alarmed" by the possibility that their new house might be Gothic.

The Classical derivatives were rooted in the glorious Renaissance, when men were measured not by the earnestness of their religious devotions, but by the success of their endeavors. Profit-motivated Americans thought the Classical said more of the things they wanted to hear, so most of the houses built in the years after the Civil War were clothed in one of the Italian styles. The field was broad enough to admit a new competitor, however, so the Second Empire Style sailed the ocean, tipped its Mansard hat, and joined the fray.

Independence - 313 3rd Street S.E.
This house displays the irregular floorplan and decorative brackets of the Italianate Style. It might have been built in the 1870s.

Ames - 829 Douglas - 1872. The window caps, hipped roof, and sidehall entrance are all characteristic of the Italianate townhouse.

Independence - 613 1st Avenue N.E. Having chosen to build on a modest scale, the first owner of this cottage was not modest enough to forgo the usual Italianate treatment. A construction date in the 1870s is likely.

Mechanicsville - 616 E. First Street - 1870. The Mansard roof does not enclose a full story. Instead, the dormer windows bisect the roof line and are flanked by console panels. Architects used this technique to squeeze the Mansard look into a compact format. The classical porch is a later addition.

Indianola - E. Salem Street - c. 1873. Here's another intriguing combination. The shape of the house and the placement of windows are reminiscent of the Federal Style, but the window caps are Italianate.

Northwood - 907 1st Avenue S. - c. 1870-74. The angled porch entrance appears to be a later addition. The gable ends are Gothic.

Dow City - 1872-74. If you lived well out on the open range in the days before barbed wire, and if you made a few dollars raising crops and livestock, this is the kind of house you might have built. Restored by volunteers, the Dow House is now a museum.

Fort Madison - 804 Avenue E - 1870. The original design gained a Queen Anne porch about 30 years later.

Davenport - 1527 Brady Avenue - c. 1871. The windows and brackets are Italianate, but the centered gable is of uncertain lineage. A 1982 photograph shows a small entrance porch, so the full-width veranda is a modern addition.

Anamosa - 1872. This late version of the Italian Villa commands a hill east of town. An engraving from the 1875 Historical Atlas of Iowa shows that the current porch is a later addition. In honor of its builder, it is now the Colonel Shaw bed-and-breakfast inn.

Second Empire *Thoroughly Modern 17th Century Baroque*

Architect Francois Mansart (1598-1666) was employed by the French royal family to design churches and palaces. He got the royal boot after quarreling with Louis XIV, gave Christopher Wren a few ideas on how to rebuild London after the Great Fire, and passed into history with a roof named in his honor. Of course he did not actually invent the thing – it was Italian – but he gave the double-pitched roof a boost and got credit in the books.

The revival of the Mansard roof began as a perfectly rational solution to the architectural problem of what to do with the attic. Its steep lines, pierced by round-headed dormer windows, made the top floor habitable, providing head room as well as style. Iowa's governors have proved this functionality by agreeing to live on the third floor of Terrace Hill. That famous house, donated to the state by the Hubbell family, is characterized in books of national scope as America's premier example of the Second Empire Style.

The year 1841 saw the first re-introduction of the Mansard roof on a prominent French building. In 1849 a London mansion was executed in the new French style, followed in 1851 by the Great Western Hotel in London. The first Mansard house in America was a New York mansion built in 1850 by a Danish-born architect who had studied in Paris.

In 1852, Napoleon III, nephew of the original Bonaparte, decided that his constitutionally-limited term as Prince-President was not enough, so he dismissed the French assembly and made himself Emperor. Louis Napoleon wanted to renew the splendors of his uncle's reign, so he laid ambitious plans for the rebuilding of Paris. The Louvre – a sort of government center, palace, art gallery, and museum rolled into one – had been modified over a period of 400 years without a coherent plan. Louis decided to connect it with the nearby Tuileries Palace, the traditional domicile of French monarchs. New work began in 1853 with the Mansard roof as the unifying design element.

The centuries-old timber and plaster houses of medieval Paris, packed together in narrow alleys, were soon swept away. Visitors to the Paris Expositions of 1855 and 1867 saw new construction projects on radial streets laid out by Baron Haussmann, the emperor's city planner. Broad boulevards were flanked by large blocks of flats with shops and

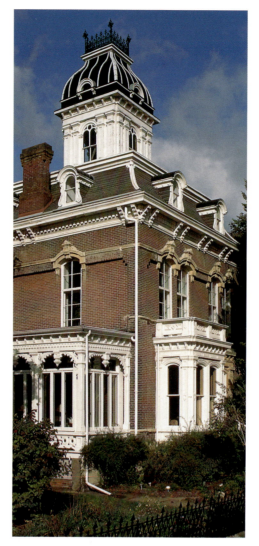

Dubuque - 1375 Locust Street - c. 1870-73. A genuine mansion by any standard, the Ryan House was designed by Chicago architect John Van Osdel. The porch on the south side was added about 1890.

Des Moines - 2300 Grand Avenue - 1867-1869. Terrace Hill was built and furnished by pioneer banker Benjamin Franklin Allen at an estimated cost of $250,000 – a truly remarkable sum in the days when a working man's wage was a dollar a day. Chicago architect William Boyington chose a style that one newspaper called "Americanized Italian with a Mansard roof." Preparation of the site on a hill west of town began in 1866 and plans for the 20-room mansion were unveiled in May 1867. During construction, a painter tumbled from the 90-foot tower but was back on the job a few days later.

To celebrate its completion the Allens held a lavish party on their 15th wedding anniversary, January 29, 1869. A $6,000 dinner was served to 600 well-attired guests – a memorable event for a prairie town with a population of only 7,000. Reporters heaped paragraphs of praise on the professional musicians, the out-of-town caterer, and the $2,000 floral display. The Register noted: "The drawing rooms of gorgeous New York, elegant Boston or stately Philadelphia are never graced with more brilliant-appearing ladies than the charming ones that thronged these parlors."

Six years later, after a move to Chicago, Allen's empire collapsed and he was forced into bankruptcy. His wife Arathusa died in 1877 at the age of 40, reportedly driven insane by fears that creditors were pursuing her. Before it was over, the liquidation of Allen's assets was carried all the way to the U.S. Supreme Court. At the time of his death in 1915, Allen owned a fruit farm in California.

In 1884 the home was purchased for $60,000 by Frederick Marion Hubbell, a businessman destined for even greater wealth and fame. Hubbell died in 1930 at the age of 91, but his son Grover lived in the mansion until 1956. Then the old house stood empty – a ghostly remnant of a bygone age.

In 1972 a 35-member state commission recommended that the house be converted into a public museum, with living quarters for the Governor and his family on the third floor. By 1974 it was ringed with scaffolds as workmen began the long-awaited restoration. There was considerable debate in the legislature about the cost, but work continued and Terrace Hill was opened to the public in July 1978.

cafes below, all sporting the new Mansard roof. When examples were publicized in the British architectural press, the style immediately jumped the Atlantic and was taken up with great enthusiasm by American designers. What we now call Second Empire was then usually defined as the "Modern Style." To the French it was a revival of 17th century Baroque decor, but to unfettered Americans it was entirely new.

The Mansard roof came in four basic configurations. The concave bell-shaped curve was the most popular domestic choice, but the bulging convex curve often appeared on public buildings. The S-shaped ogee curve was the most difficult to execute, and the flat-surfaced Mansard was the cheapest. The steep slope was usually topped with an overhanging cornice, above which was mounted a pyramidal roof shallow enough to be nearly invisible from the street.

The Mansardic style encompassed the Italianate vocabulary, so that Classically styled brackets were ranged about the cornices and doorways. Often the only departure from the earlier formula was a Mansard cap on an Italian tower. The French roof was so inherently combinable, it fostered a wide range of eclectic treatments.

One of the leading adopters of Second Empire was Alfred Mullett, Supervising Architect of the U.S. Treasury from 1865 to 1875. He commissioned dozens of new federal buildings, especially courthouses and post offices. So closely was the Mansard associated with government work that the product was sometimes referred to as the "General Grant Style." Ulysses S. was President from 1869 to 1877, years that spanned the height of the Mansard vogue.

Clinton - 538-540 10th Avenue S. - c. 1869. In the years after the Civil War, the Mansard roof was frequently added to the already popular Italianate tower. Though much altered, this house retains its wrought-iron roof cresting.

Lansing - 611 Dodge Street - c. 1870. The multi-layered Second Empire Style sometimes displayed Mansard roofs on wings of different heights.

Dubuque - 11th and Main. The Second Empire Style was well suited to the compact arrangement of urban row houses.

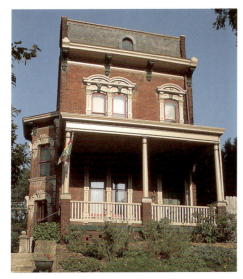

Burlington - 613 N. 5th Street - 1870. Perched high above the street, this Mansard-roofed townhouse is squeezed onto a narrow lot. The complex design of the classical window is highlighted by a new set of colors.

Dubuque - 1640 Main Street - 1878. Now a funeral home, this elegant residence is one of Iowa's best examples of the Second Empire Style.

1873

One Sunday morning in June 1873 a farmer named Thomas Barry was invited to join a party of German immigrants on their way to church. There was no road in the vicinity, so the settlers steered their wagon across open prairie toward Hospers, a small village in northwest Iowa.

Years later, Josephine Barry Donovan wrote an account of that day for an issue of the *Palimpsest*. The article does not say so, but the author must have been Mr. Barry's daughter. With an ironic twist, she set the stage for his grim recollection.

"The sun was well up in the cloudless blue sky, causing the drops of dew to shine in the soft green grass mottled with prairie flowers… Meadow larks, like an orchestra of flutes, greeted us with their jubilant song."

Moved by the beauty of his surroundings, Barry called out:

"Isn't this wonderful?" They looked at me rather blankly so I hesitated a little and ventured, "Schön, sehr schön, nicht wahr?" and spread my arms over

Clermont - 1874. On a hill overlooking the town, future governor William Larrabee built a handsome estate and called it Montauk. Milwaukee architect Edward Townsend Mix chose the decorative Italian Palazzo Style, but the owner wrote on the blueprint: "Want all carved work left off." It was built from locally made brick, featured a central steam heating plant, and cost $20,000. Montauk is now a museum operated by the state of Iowa.

Mount Pleasant - 408 N. Broadway - 1874. This Mansard-roofed house features all the usual Italianate elements, including decorative window caps. Like many old mansions, it is now a funeral home.

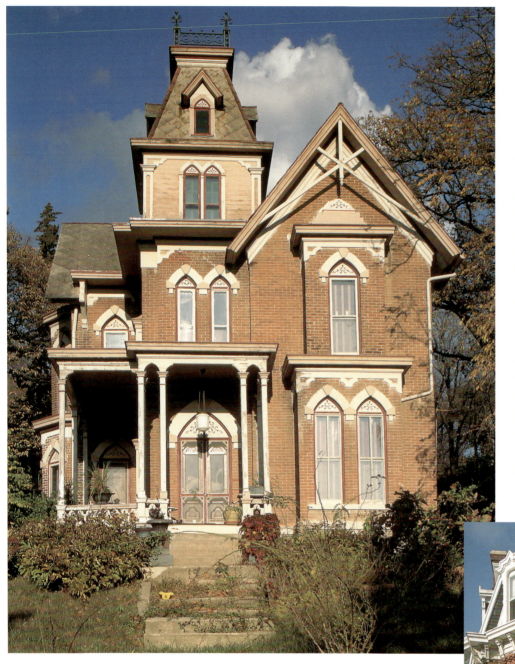

other mystified. "Der jüngste Tag," one man shouted and began to pray. The cloud broadened out and settled lower as it drew near: the noise became deafening."

As the farmers were rolling slowly across the prairie on their way to church, a few counties to the south, others were streaming by at a more rapid pace. An Englishman named William Fraser Rae was among the first to traverse the continent by rail, a journey made possible by the driving of the golden spike at Promontory, Utah in May 1869. His ensuing yarn, filled with practical advice for European travelers, was titled *Westward By Rail*.

Seated in the elegantly appointed drawing room of a Pullman Palace Car, Mr. Rae rode the Chicago and Northwestern line five hundred miles to the eastern terminus of the Union Pacific at Omaha. As his train rattled across the Iowa prairies, the writer looked out at a landscape still largely empty, so vacant in fact that the Iowa leg of the ocean-

the land. They all assented, "Ja," but one settler who had seen June prairies before edged up more closely and said, "Ja, schön, but you can't eat it."

Halfway to their destination the settlers observed a large black cloud high in the west.

"...from which came an ominous sound. The apparition moved directly toward us, its dark appearance became more and more terrifying, and the sound changed to a deep hum. At first we thought a cyclone was upon us. The oxen stopped and we all stared at each

Council Bluffs - 151 Park Avenue - 1877. A Mansard tower contrasts with a Stick Style truss at the gable.

Dubuque - 1611 W. Main. The Mansard roof added to the top floor's usable space.

linking adventure merited only six of his 391 pages.

"On either side, as far as the horizon, a few farmhouses alone serve to break the monotony of the prospect. To these vast tracts the epithet which Homer affixed to the sea may not inaptly be applied. They are literally "unharvested," awaiting the touch of industry to yield up their teeming treasures. The long, rank grass which waves on the surface, rots for lack of a mower to gather it in, or is converted into dust and ashes when the spark falling from the passing locomotive, or thrown by the heedless wanderer, kindles the flame which no human power can extinguish.

"The spectacle of a prairie on fire is one of infinite grandeur. For miles on every side the air is heavy with volumes of stifling smoke, and the ground reddened with hissing and rushing fire. The beholder can with difficulty apprehend the possibility of the mass of flame being quenched till the entire

Marshalltown - 503 W. Main Street - c. 1875. A stylish Mansard roof tops the short tower of this otherwise Italianate house. The columned porch was probably added around the turn of the century.

Storm Lake - Lake and 3rd Streets - 1875. Most houses in the Second Empire Style were three stories tall, but the builders of smaller dwellings also savored the new French roof.

country had become a barren and blackened waste. Much depends upon the strength of the wind as well as the quarter from which it blows."

Was it a prairie fire, then, that imperilled the settlers that Sunday morning? No, the sinking cloud was more substantial than smoke. Said Barry:

"When it was directly over us it looked like a heavy storm of black flakes, the dark particles singling out and becoming more defined in shape as they descended. We heard the buzzing; we saw the shining wings, the long bodies, the legs. The grasshoppers – the scourge of the prairie – were upon us."

Thus began the onslaught. The ravenous horde consumed virtually every organic substance – corn, wheat, oats, vegetables

Iowa City - 906 E. College - 1875. Now a sorority house, this roomy Mansard has long adorned the college town.

in the garden, even the laundry hung to dry on clothes lines. Tall cottonwoods turned to shimmering skeletons as every green leaf and tender twig was rapidly engulfed. The insects even fell upon sheep and stripped the wool from their backs.

"In alighting, they circled in myriads about you, beating against everything animate or inanimate, driving into open doors and windows, heaping about your feet and around your buildings, while their jaws were constantly at work biting and testing all things in seeking what they could devour… The grasshoppers transformed the prairie into a barren world. Only the coarsest dry grass remained."

In two hours time the brutal work was finished. The hoppers took wing to press their attack on the next farm, and the next. In the days that followed, swarms of grasshoppers blanketed most of Lyon, Sioux, O'Brien, and Osceola counties, and made scattered assaults on fifteen others.

The permanent range of the Rocky Mountain Locust, known to entomologists as *Caloptenus spretus*, did not include the state of Iowa. They bred along the rivers and grassy slopes east of the Continental Divide in the territories of Montana, Idaho, Wyoming, Colorado, and Nebraska. From time to time, obscure climatic forces drove huge swarms east in search of food. Travelers reported sighting grasshopper clouds in Minnesota as early as 1818, and five Iowa counties were invaded in 1857. At that time, however, there were few permanent residents to take note of their passings.

The first widespread loss of crops occurred in 1867, when grasshopper swarms were reported from the Missouri

Traer - 501 Walnut - c. 1879. The symmetry of this boxy Italianate house is relieved by a wraparound porch. When the photograph was taken, balustered railings between the posts had been removed for repair.

Dubuque - 1491 Main Street - c. 1870s. Architects of the Second Empire Style seldom chose to build with stone, so this is a rare specimen. Sharply angled sunlight is required to bring out the shallow relief of the surface decoration.

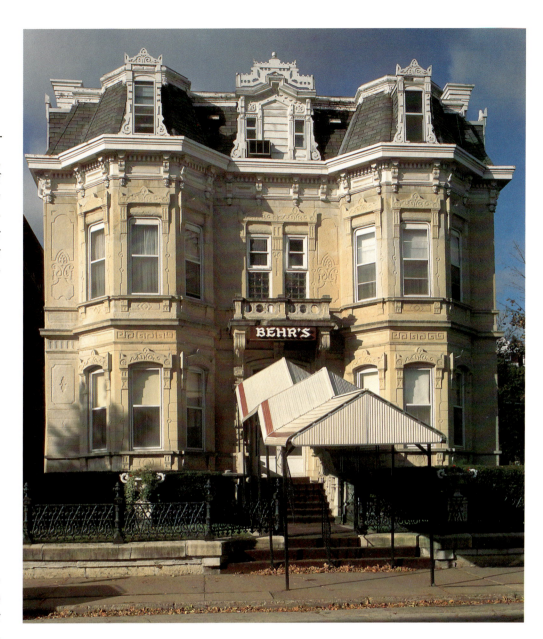

River east to Ft. Dodge, Jefferson, and Adel. Some areas were stripped of vegetation while others were scarcely touched. The year 1873 marked the onset of the most calamitous grasshopper infestations. In November of that year the town of Sibley issued an impassioned appeal for economic relief.

"The most of the settlers came here last spring with little or no means, and depending entirely on their efforts during the summer to carry them through the winter… There are hundreds of families who have not sufficient clothing, and know not where the bread that they will eat ten day hence is coming from… We, therefore, appeal to the liberal Christian hearted people of the State for assistance in the shape of money, clothing, fuel, and staple articles of food."

Many communities in the more prosperous regions of the state responded to these pleas for charity, and grasshopper parties became something of a fad. Hats were passed for the collection of coins, and ladies' committees assembled shipments of clothing, bedding, and other household articles. Railroads that touched the region promised, for a short time only, free transportation of commodities.

When the state legislature met in January 1874, Governor Carpenter delivered a compelling speech.

"During the last two years there has been a constant stream of immigration

Waterloo - 306 Washington Street - 1878. Another variation on the Italianate theme, this unusually horizontal design features sheet-metal window caps. It now belongs to the Waterloo Women's Club.

pouring into the counties in the northwestern portion of the State. So rapid has been this influx, that in counties where three years ago there was scarcely a human habitation there are today from two to three thousand inhabitants. When it is considered that a large proportion of these settlers went into this country with very limited means, in order to take advantage of the homestead law, and that under the most favorable circumstances they must have undergone severe deprivations and hardships, it is scarcely a matter of surprise that, when there is added to these facts an unusual shortness of crops, there should be great want and distress."

The governor remarked that settlers had

Corning - 906 6th Street - c. 1877-1881. Here is a rarity – an Italianate house with wooden window trim. Real estate abstracts never reveal when a house was built, only when a parcel was sold. An increase in value suggests that the house was added to the property during a four-year interval.

Osage - 803 State Street - c. 1877. This Italianate house is decorated with wooden roof brackets and cast-iron window caps.

48

been lured to these "sparsely timbered counties" on the promise that a railroad would soon link them to sources of food and fuel. Delays in completing the McGregor and Sioux City line had left them stranded.

The pattern of prairie settlement has no parallel in our century, so to understand the dynamics of immigration we must again consult our train traveler. From his Pullman window, Mr. Rae saw rows of neatly planted trees and supposed it must be a nursery garden.

"A fellow-traveller who knew the country and its customs, told me that my supposition was erroneous. The spot was the chosen site of a future city. It is thus that speculators plan out and prepare the way for the settlement of uninhabited tracts of suitable land. Not only do they plant the trees destined to overshadow the footpaths on which unborn children will play, but they also give names to the streets, and even set apart sites for imaginary buildings. All these things are carefully noted in a map which is shown to the seekers of new abodes. They buy lots where their fancy dictates, and sometimes find on arriving to take possession that they are the first and the only inhabitants."

And so they came to settle the prairie, and suffered the grasshoppers in consequence.

At first, newspapers in the northwestern part of the state did not report the unfolding drama. News of the plague might keep immigrants away and forestall the region's economic development. Fields of waving grain were abundant, the writers insisted. There was no reason not to settle here. When finally forced to admit the scope of the calamity, the papers drew favorable comparisons with the unfortunate of other regions. One newspaper reported that in the states of Kansas and Nebraska, 40,000 people were left destitute by the grasshopper rampage.

Meanwhile, land speculators gathered up choice parcels at bargain prices.

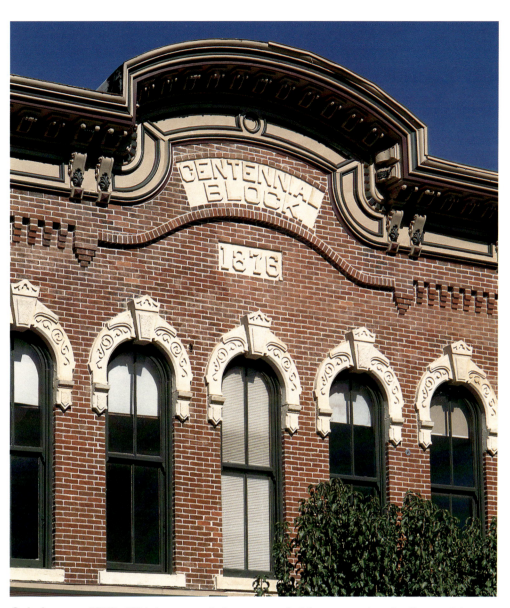

Oskaloosa - 1876. With its stone window caps and elaborate cornice, the Centennial Block is one of the finest Italianate storefronts of the period.

Cedar Falls

Some farmers, having sold all the livestock to keep their families alive, simply nailed shut the doors of their shacks and walked away. Others sought out the "sharpers" to take whatever money was offered for quit-claim deeds. In due course the legislature impaneled a "Special Committee on Destitution" to explore the stricken counties. The observers reported:

"None of their residences are extravagant, and seldom embrace more than one room. A majority of them are neat, though rough, having little furniture aside from such articles as the man of the house could manufacture. Some of the houses are made of sod, with straw roofs, in which floors other than the hard ground may be absent. A few pounds of flour, or a little meal, with possibly a little pork of some kind,

Winterset. Covered bridges are not the only attractions in Madison County. A variety of storefront windows look out at the courthouse square.

Winterset - c. 1870s. Some decorative window caps were produced by pouring cement slurry into a mold, but others appear to have been cut from stone with a mallet and chisel. Only close inspection can detect the difference. The style shown here may be unique to this building.

---

generally comprised the stock of provisions – with no hope beyond the good hearts of the more fortunate people of Iowa for fresh supplies."

Economic conditions were made worse in September 1873 by a financial panic that swept the nation's investment markets. Jay Cooke, a wealthy speculator, had gone too far and many had followed him, including Iowa's B.F. Allen, owner of Terrace Hill. In the ensuing crash,

Prairie City. Most storefronts measured 22 to 25 feet – just wide enough for three decorative windows.

farmers everywhere suffered. The value of corn dropped to twelve cents a bushel and eggs were selling for a nickel a dozen. In these circumstances, private charities struggled to meet the needs of their neighbors. Despite the difficulties, substantial relief was gladly offered and gratefully accepted.

Year after year the grasshoppers continued their attacks. Cold weather killed the adults, but in the Spring the ground was alive with voracious larvae. The new generation hatched in May, so that emerging crops were instantly ruined. In desperation, farmers splashed kerosene on the ground and set fire to their fields. Others tried plowing the eggs under in hopes that hatching larvae could not reach the surface. In eight weeks the hoppers gained their wings and began marauding, their ranks reinforced by fresh legions from the west. The only economic salvation was that herds of hogs and flocks of poultry gorged themselves on the bugs and were thereby fattened for market.

In 1876 a governors' conference was held at Omaha, and though scientists had few remedies to offer, 10,000 copies of the proceedings were published. In the end, cold, wet weather did more to end the scourge than all the efforts of mankind. It was also thought that mother nature, responding finally to the tipping of her scales, had afflicted the hoppers with parasites. Insect populations dropped in 1877 and 1878, and the last was seen of them in 1879. As soon as the hoppers were gone and the tracks were laid, northwest Iowa enjoyed the long awaited boom.

Meanwhile, immigrants continued pouring into the state at the rate of more than 50,000 a year. A generation earlier, pioneers had fashioned most of their own household commodities, but now there were stores in the towns where

Avoca

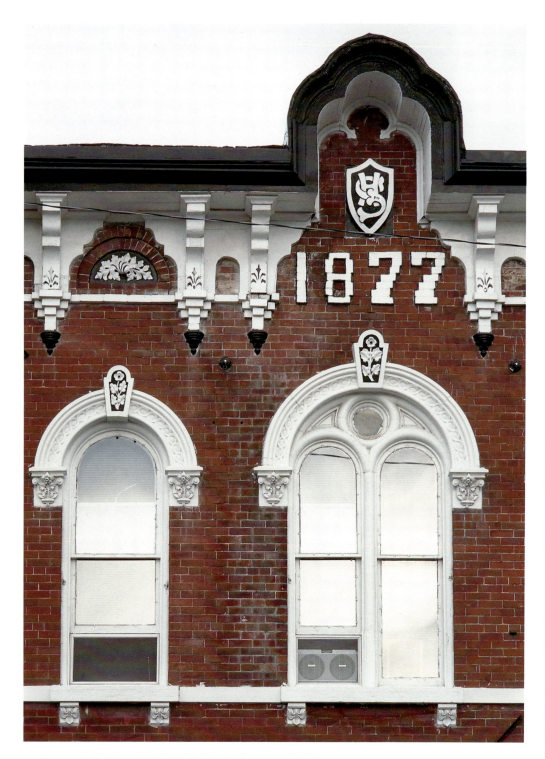

Council Bluffs - 509-511 S. Main Street - 1877. The window caps are metal, but the cornice is wood. The building is part of the Haymarket Commercial Historic District.

Albia - 1869.
Osage - 1872. The first window decorations were ornate cast-iron caps. Earlier commercial buildings usually featured plain stone lintels above the windows.

Dubuque - 160-185 Main Street - c. 1870s. Victorian builders did not think it important to align their windows with those of the adjoining buildings.

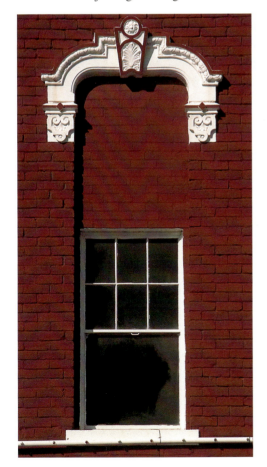

Red Oak

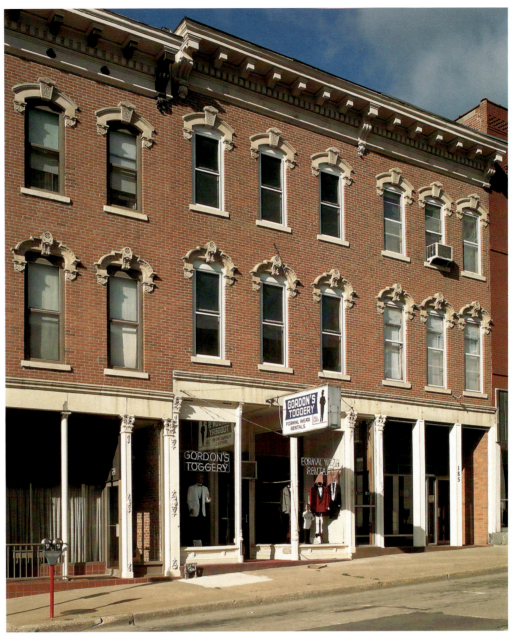

hard-earned dollars could buy manufactured products. Like the captains of industry who were putting up mansions, the humble retailer also needed an appropriate architecture.

The 1875 *Historical Atlas of Iowa* contained engraved illustrations of banks, hotels, stores, and factories, some four stories tall, and most built of solid Iowa brick. Countless decorative elements were displayed, some produced locally and others imported from the East. In the final quarter of the 19th century the streetscape of small-town Iowa was literally set in concrete as town squares were filled with blocks of handsome commercial buildings.

In the larger cities of Iowa these buildings have been demolished and forgotten. Many were systematically exterminated in the 1950s in a frenzy of "urban renewal." Only a few isolated structures remain to suggest the original architectural atmosphere of those streets. But in the county-seat towns, where the dual pressures of slum clearance and rising land value have not destroyed them, hundreds of old storefronts are still alive and well.

Ottumwa - 224 E. Main Street. There were many prefabricated window caps from which to choose, so some builders employed more than one style.

Italianate Stores —— *Decorative Cornices and Window Caps*

Architectural historians generally use the term *High Victorian Italianate* to characterize commercial buildings of the 1870s, though they admit that the origins are obscure. Rows of identically styled windows can be easily traced to the Italian palazzos of Florence and Rome, but the forms of 19th century American decoration have few direct antecedents. One authority notes that use of the word "vernacular" is a confession of ignorance, but if ignorant, one is certainly in good company.

The predominant form of expression was the decorative window cap, sometimes called a hood molding or lintel. The tops of Renaissance window openings were either perfectly round or perfectly square, but in 1840 an English architect named Charles Robert Cockerell introduced the stilted segmental arch. In this form, the top of the window is slightly curved, but the decorative elements wrap around the opening and descend vertically. Once this break with convention had found its niche, new window treatments were routinely invented.

Prior to the Civil War the principal decorative device was a piece of cast iron bolted to a wall above a window, but even that was rare. By 1875 window caps were being produced in countless styles, and in a variety of materials. Some were molded from concrete in local building-supply yards, while others

---

Pella. Identical window caps have been treated to different color schemes. The building on the right has its openings squeezed together to make room for a turret.

Manning. Load bearing cast iron columns offer another opportunity for multi-colored effects.

Jefferson - 1874. Along with gargoyles and other mythical figures, Gothic artists often decorated their cathedrals with human faces, if decorated is the right word. Do the classical looking faces in this design have some meaning, or is it just another ornamental form? Identical window caps were installed on buildings in at least two other towns.

Dubuque - 13th & Central. The window treatments seen here are remarkably close to the Renaissance prototypes. The assembled pieces appear to be made of terra cotta.

were made of terra cotta – a kiln-fired clay similar to brick. Some window caps were fashioned as a single unit, while others were installed as a set of adjoining pieces.

When decorative storefronts look fresh and crisp after more than a century, the substance is usually galvanized iron. Decorative cornices across the tops of walls were sometimes built of masonry or wood, but sheet metal was the preferred material. The first stamping

machines, called cornice brakes, were developed in the 1840s.

Because they could be produced in 8-foot sections, metal cornices were manufactured long before the machinists were ready to try their hands at the more difficult shapes of window caps. In examples from the 1870s one often sees metal cornices in combi-

Wilton. This is how zinc-coated window caps look when not covered with paint.

nation with decorative masonry, but by 1880 complete sheet-iron facades had captured the market.

Des Moines had its own sheet-iron factory at a comparatively early date. In 1878, L.G. Comparet and Jacob Stark – "Manufacturers of Galvanized Iron Cornice, Window Caps, and Chimney Tops" – erected a handsome three-story building at 315 Walnut Street and covered the exterior with a lavish display of their decorative products. None of the styles shown in this building's illustration is known to survive.

The galvanizing process involved hot-dipping thin sheets of iron or steel in vats of molten zinc. The zinc coating prevented rust from forming on the surface, but paint did not adhere well and often peeled off in large strips after a few years of exposure. Modern paints are better, but patches of dull gray on many store fronts attest to the continuing difficulties associated with maintaining these luxuriantly detailed surfaces.

Pure zinc was often used for the casting of complex designs. One usually finds that straight members, such as

Clarinda - c. 1870. This town-square building was demolished in 1996. When photographed, a portion of the cornice had been removed, revealing the brick and wood underneath. The window caps appeared to have been molded from a cement slurry containing a high ratio of sand.

Independence - 1st Street E.

Red Oak. When concrete window caps are seen in conjunction with a metal cornice, the store was usually built in the 1870s.

embossed panels and flat window sills, attract a magnet, but that three-dimensional decorative pieces do not.

The use of tin as a coating was largely restricted to roofing materials. Thomas Jefferson installed tin-plated iron sheets on the roof of Monticello about 1800.

At ground-floor entrances, large expanses of plate glass were made possible by slender cast-iron columns. Decorative iron fronts were produced in the East as early as 1825, but pre-fabrication of standardized pieces did not get properly started until 1849. Competitors James Bogardus and Daniel Badger of New York were the first to make standardized iron fronts for shipment to distant building sites. By 1855, Dubuque had an iron foundry capable of producing architectural columns for the local market.

Bedford. This southern Iowa town is home to an interesting collection of metal cornices.

Iowa City - 127 E. College - 1878. One source lists 1883 as the date of construction, but a series of old newspaper articles prove that it was built between August 15 and November 6, 1878. Because it was designed by a local architect, the stamped-metal decor may be entirely unique.

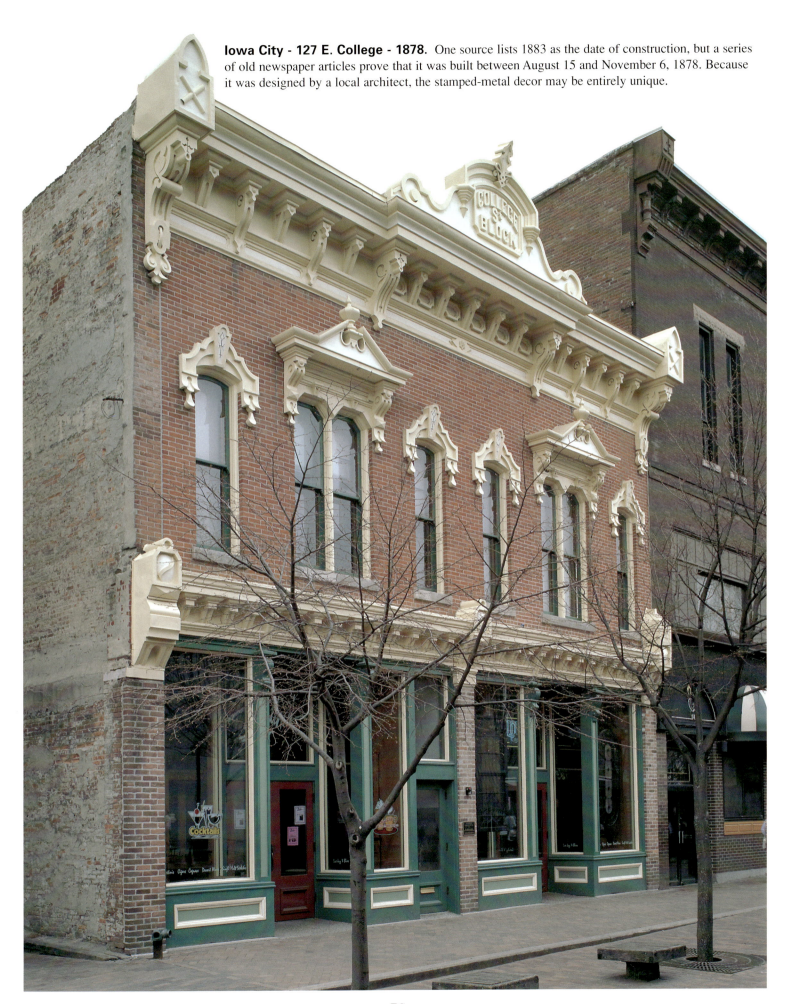

Cedar Falls - 1017 Washington Street - c. 1878-1884. Built sometime during a six year span, this eclectically styled house is both Gothic and Italianate. The pointed spire is found on houses in other states, so the plan was probably taken from a pattern book.

Pella - 714 Independence Street - 1880. This pleasant cottage resembles those built during the 1850's Gothic Revival. Its late arrival on the scene suggests that people were still reading A.J. Downing's books.

1880

The federal census of 1880 found that Iowa's population had grown to 1,624,615. Nearly a million new faces had appeared in just twenty years, and though there were a few marshes left to drain, most of Iowa's 36 million acres had been settled.

Wheat was the easiest crop for early settlers to grow as it could be sowed and harvested without machinery. Iowa's output peaked in 1875 with three million acres planted and 44 million bushels harvested. As more land was opened for settlement, wheat production moved west to Nebraska, Kansas, and the Dakotas. Corn was better suited to Iowa's deep black soil, and more resistant to the chinch bugs that periodically ruined the wheat crop.

Most of the corn grown in Iowa was marketed on the hoof. In 1880 the inventory of cattle topped two million, ranking Iowa second only to Texas in beef production. For sheer numbers, though, there was nothing to compare with pork. The first mongrel hogs were "long legged, sharp nosed, slab sided, fence despising races," but by 1880 farmers were breeding Suffolks, Berkshires, Yorkshires, and Poland Chinas, and their numbers totalled six million. Because they were easy to raise and could be herded to railheads, hogs were called "mortgage lifters."

The development of Iowa's livestock industry paralleled the expansion of the railroads. By 1880, five major lines connected the Mississippi and Missouri Rivers, and dozens of spur lines ran north and south. Among the 38 states, Iowa ranked fifth with 5,235 miles of track, and no home was more than 25 miles from a rail line.

Livestock production was also aided by the invention of barbed wire. In 1874, plants in Iowa and Illinois produced five tons of the new wire, but two years later the output had grown to nearly 1,500 tons. The era of the open range was rapidly drawing to a close.

Though most Iowans lived on farms, by 1880 the agrarian population had stopped growing. It remained for the cities and towns to absorb another 1.3 million souls. Des Moines, with 22,408 citizens to its credit, was the largest settlement.

Lumber milling was Iowa's largest non-agricultural industry. By 1860, 540 saw mills were cutting indigenous walnut, maple, and oak into studs for frame houses, though most such enterprises served strictly local markets. The native hardwoods of Iowa were unsuitable for large-scale homebuilding, so the white pine forests along the Wisconsin and St. Croix Rivers were tapped for their seemingly inexhaustible supplies of timber. Trees were felled in the Winter and hauled on horse-drawn sleds over the hard ground to the banks of rivers. In Spring the logs were floated down-

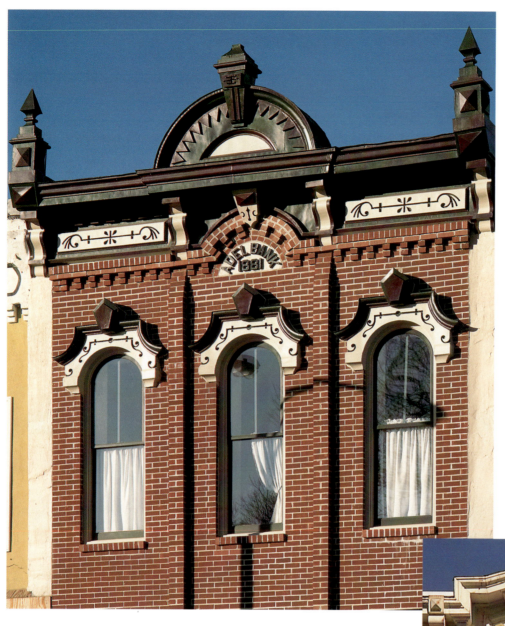

soon be acclaimed America's largest producer of finished lumber. Thanks to mill owners such as Benjamin Hershey, Muscatine held a respectable 11% of the trade and ranked third behind Davenport. On June 5, 1879, Hershey's steamboat landed what was said to be the largest raft ever brought down the river. Measuring 310 by 535 feet, it was three-and-a-half times the size of a football field. The record did not hold up for long. Soon it was possible to see rafts nearly twice that size on the Mississippi.

Iowa's lumber industry peaked about 1890 when 560 million board feet were cut and sold. Soon after the turn of the century the inexhaustible northern forests were exhausted, so the mill owners switched to imported Southern pine and Pacific fir.

Milling was not limited to dimensional lumber for wall studs and rafters. As early as 1855, Burlington had a planing mill, four sash and door factories, and a shingle splitter. By 1880 the list of products included banisters, newel posts, porch brackets, and – most notably – scroll-sawed gable ends. The stream and lashed into booms on the Mississippi.

A typical log raft was made up of "strings" measuring 16 by 400 feet, bound together with windlass and chain and fixed with pins through overlaid poles. Atop this undulating surface were mounted the cook's shack and crude sleeping shelters for a crew of from 20 to 35. To negotiate sandbars the raftsmen steered with 30-foot oars at an average speed of two miles an hour. In later years, steamboats were used to speed the rafts downstream.

In 1878 a Dubuque newspaper reported the seasonal passing of more than 700 rafts. Many were destined for Clinton, which already owned 40% of the state's milling business and would

Adel - 1881. There is almost no historical evidence to indicate how galvanized store fronts were originally painted. Modern multi-color schemes look perfectly appropriate, so one is tempted to speculate that the effect may be reasonably authentic.

Monticello - 1881. Brick masons produced decorative wall patterns to complement the sheet-metal elements.

era of manufactured ornament was at hand, and competing styles of Classical and Gothic decoration were freely mixed with original American designs. For the remainder of the Victorian era, wood was king.

Throughout the 19th century, cultural critics called for the development of a truly American architecture. Patriotic writers thought that the proliferation of derivative European styles cast doubts on America's inventive spirit. One pattern-book designer of the day sought to explain how things had been going. Henry Hudson Holly published *Modern Dwellings in Town and Country in 1878.*

"Architecture is a comparatively new art in this country, and has had but little earnest and intelligent study; so we cannot be said to have any styles and

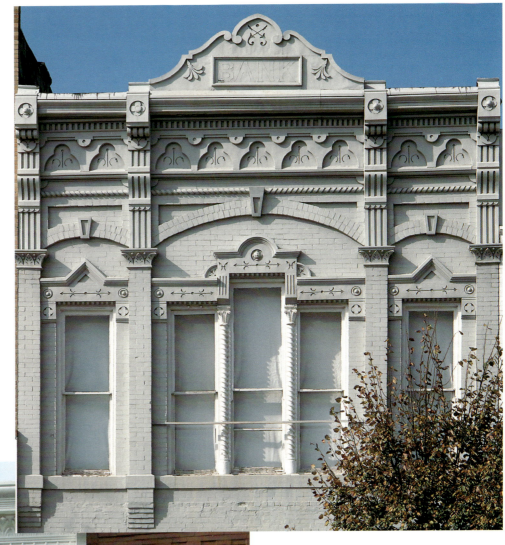

Clarinda - 1880-1884. This county seat town is home to a good collection of metal storefronts from the 1880s.

systems peculiarly our own. In the absence of such, we have been too apt to use, inappropriately, the orders of foreign nations, which express the especial needs of those countries, and those alone. Yet out of our necessities there have grown certain idiosyncrasies of building which point toward an American style. Doubtless we may introduce from abroad methods of design which meet our requirements, but we must not hesitate to eliminate those portions for which we have no use, or to make such additions as our circumstances demand."

As willing as Holly may have been to discard inappropriate models, the drawings in his book show that he had cast off very little of the latest import.

In the early 1870s two new stylistic forces appeared, both of which were the product of prominent English

Davenport - 1208 Main Street - 1881-84. Though the French roof was losing popularity, newer styles had not been fully accepted. If you wanted to build an updisputed mansion it was best to stick with a recognized commodity.

designers. The two groundbreakers for whom everything was misnamed were Charles Locke Eastlake (1836-1906) and Richard Norman Shaw (1831-1912).

Like A.J. Davis before him, Charles Eastlake was an illustrator who at an early age won praise for his structural drawings. After an apprenticeship with Philip Hardwick, a noted English architect, he traveled in Europe for three years and became a devoted admirer of ancient medieval buildings. Though Eastlake had the usual qualifications, he never earned a living as an architect. One source says that he "designed a few houses," but no specific buildings are listed to his credit.

In 1866, Eastlake was elected Secretary of the Royal Institute of British Architects, a post he held for 12 years. It was this occupation to which one biographer says his "professional career as an architect was confined." From 1878 to 1898, as Keeper of the National Gallery, he arranged and classified Britain's historic paintings. But it was as a popular author of home-decorating advice that Eastlake won lasting fame.

In 1868 he published *Hints on Household Taste*, a book intended to improve the domestic arts. An American edition appeared in 1872, immediately became a best seller, and went through six printings in as many years. Eastlake illustrated his book with original designs for tables, chairs, bookcases, wash stands, sideboards, bedsteads, and chests of drawers. He renounced glue – only pegged joints were "honest" – and condemned varnish and veneer. Though Eastlake sought to elevate the common taste, his designs were often characterized by critics as massive, ponderous, and graceless. In 1877 critic Harriet Spofford wrote:

"The book met a great want. Not a young marrying couple who read English were to be found without 'Hints on Household Taste' in their hands, and all its dicta were accepted as gospel truths. They hung their pictures and their curtains just as Mr. Eastlake said they should; laid their carpets, colored their walls, hinged their doors, arranged their china... all after Mr. Eastlake's own heart.

"Presently there arose a demand for furniture in the "Eastlake style." The upholsterers, with whom Mr. Eastlake had made quarrel in his pages, denied that there was any such style... The demand, however, was one which obliged the upholsterers to pocket their grudge, and if there were no Eastlake style, to invent one."

Keokuk - 226 Morgan - 1880-81. The designer of this Second Empire house compensated for the use of plain window caps by adding decorative pediments to the square-cut dormers.

To satisfy fad-hungry customers, American furniture builders generally laid on more fussy decoration than the namesake could abide. In a later edition of his book Eastlake remarked:

"I find American tradesmen continually advertising what they are pleased to call 'Eastlake' furniture, with the production of which I have had nothing whatever to do, and for the taste of which I should be very sorry to be considered responsible."

Because furniture and architecture had often run on parallel tracks, it was inevitable that Eastlake's ideas should be associated with the design of houses. Soon craftsmen were fashioning porch posts to resemble the table legs they saw in his drawings. To many, Eastlake's designs looked Gothic, though the author was quick to clarify the label.

"Some critics have taken exception to what they not unjustifiably call my medieval predilections… It is the spirit and principles of early manufacture which I desire to see revived, and not the absolute forms in which they found embodiment."

There was no escaping the Gothic stamp, however, when in 1872 Eastlake published *A History of the Gothic Revival*. He described the book as: "An attempt to show how the taste for medieval architecture which lingered in England during the two last centuries has since been encouraged and developed." The work not only proved Eastlake a capable historian, it also cemented his link to

Montgomery County - 1882. About ten miles west of Red Oak a church and a few houses mark the site of Hawthorne, a village that no longer appears on the roadmaps. Nearby, high on a hill, B.F. Runnells built "Fairview Place." Seen through a grove of ancient gnarled pines, the long-abandoned house presented a ghostly visage. Though the slate-covered roof proved durable, wind and water brought down a portion of the limestone wall. Inside, scorched flooring was the artifact of a hobo's campfire. Until its demolition in 1997, this was Iowa's premiere Victorian ruin.

Bellevue - 301 State Street - 1881. There are four chimneys but no fireplaces – the seven-bedroom house was originally heated with stoves. Outside walls are more than two feet thick, with insulating air spaces between courses of brick. In 1980 the owners began a meticulous restoration.

Chariton - 330 S. Grand. This vernacular house offers a unique set of decorative elements that seem to hail from the 1880s.

decorative architecture.

In preparation for his second book, Eastlake surveyed a number of British architects and asked them to define their styles. Richard Norman Shaw replied that his recent country houses were rendered in the *Old English Style*. The term Old English had been commonly used since about 1830 to characterize certain rustic interpretations of Gothic, Tudor, and Elizabethan precedents, yet the importance of Norman Shaw's commissions made it all seem quite new.

Between 1866 and 1870, Shaw built sprawling manor houses for the wealthy in the English counties of Sussex and Kent. His early masterpiece, Leyswood, was poised on a rocky promontory overlooking the sea. Whereas the Gothic Revival had emphasized carved wooden ornament, the Old English Style relied on picturesque massing. Leyswood greeted the eye with a proliferation of gables, towering chimneys of sculpted brickwork, great expanses of leaded glass in iron casements, and tile hangings under the eaves.

Shaw, once the star architectural student at the Royal Academy School, had flung together a handful of elements spanning the Tudor and Stuart centuries. Some observers saw a direct line of descent from the great manor houses built during the reign of James I (1603-1625). Two of the best known were Hatfield and Bramshill, both erected in 1612. From this precedent the term *Neo-Jacobean* was coined, after Jacobus, the Latin form of James. Whatever label might be applied to him, it was clear that Shaw was not trying to recreate any precise moment, but rather to evoke an atmosphere of antique charm.

Lamoni - west on J55 - 1881. After the assassination of Joseph Smith, the founder of Mormonism, his five sons did not follow Brigham Young to Utah. In 1860, Joseph Smith III (1832-1914) became leader of the Reorganized Church of Jesus Christ of Latter Day Saints. This was one of his homes.

Mount Pleasant - 208 E. Henry - 1882. The builder of this house chose to combine the bracketed Italianate Style, nearly out of fashion, with the new ornaments of the Gingerbread Age. The porch trim is original, but the angled steps were added in the 1890s.

Mitchellville - 10150 N.E. 46th Avenue - 1881. Located a few miles east of Altoona, this attractive farm house features Italianate decorations.

Winterset - 503 E. Jefferson - 1886. This late Italianate house features a style of window cap that is often seen on storefront buildings. The brick walls were covered with stucco about 1925.

The primary visual element of the Old English style was half-timbered wall construction. In medieval times, heavy oak beams were mortised together and the open spaces were filled with whatever materials were at hand. In the most primitive examples the fill was "wattle and daub," a loosely woven curtain of tree branches cemented with mud. By the beginning of the 16th century the English were stacking bricks, called nogging, in the empty spaces and covering them with plaster, allowing the structural beams to show through. The principal decorative touch was a carved bargeboard hung from the gable, the same precedent that had been borrowed a generation earlier to launch the Gothic Revival.

Despite Eastlake's call for the honest use of materials, Shaw's fake half-timbering was a thin veneer of lumber and stucco over a solid brick wall. Adding to the antique appearance were layers of thin clay tiles overlapped like shingles, either bedded in mortar or pegged to battens across the wall face. This had been a standard method of weatherproofing the upper stories of timber-framed houses.

After carving a niche in the countryside with the Old English Style, Norman Shaw needed something more sophisticated for the city. In 1872 he startled the architectural fraternity with his design for the London office of a steamship line. New Zealand Chambers featured two-story oriolle windows – curved bays that projected above the street. The ornament came from a 17th century house in Ipswich that had been richly decorated with plaster moldings. Shaw had made

Davenport - 628 Kirkwood Blvd. - 1881. This Italianate house features an uncharacteristic dormer window in the hipped roof.

sparing use of decorative plaster, known as pargetting, on some of his country houses, but now the Renaissance craft was fully showcased.

Others were quick to adopt these new "Free Classic" themes. One colleague noted that the new style combined elements from "the time of the Jameses, Queen Anne and the early Georges" – a period of 150 years. Though they had failed to mention several intervening monarchs, the meaning was clear. Shaw and his contemporaries were eclectics who had no interest in scholarly dogma. The dons at the Royal Academy were aghast. One recent com-

Mount Vernon - 1st Street and 7th Avenue - 1884. This is one of the few Iowa houses in the so-called Stick Style. Non-structural boards simulated the half-timbered wall of the English manor house.

mentator has written that the new style "infuriated both the old Gothicists and the old Classicists, the Gothicists because it was Classic and the Classicists because it was Free."

It is not clear if Shaw was the one who first used the term "Queen Anne" to pigeonhole his work, but someone used it, and the label stuck. A few of the new buildings actually did resemble the products of Queen Anne's reign (1702-1714), but most were too eclectic to date.

For the Philadelphia Centennial Exposition of 1876, British exhibitors offered an impression of the Old English Style. To mimic the divisions of the half-

Onawa - 1106 Iowa Avenue - 1880-82. If you like a mystery, solve this one. There are more than 50 window caps and at least 100 brackets, all made of steel and zinc. Manufactured cornices conceal cleverly designed rain gutters that feed integrated downspouts. The cupola was firmly out of fashion by 1880, so why would a builder combine the latest technology with an obsolete style?

Pella - East on Hwy 163 - 1892.
None of the familiar style names can be applied to the kind of decorations seen here. Lumber milling plants turned out thousands of gable ends and ornamental pieces, but they are neither Eastlake nor Queen Anne.

Lemars - 400 2nd Avenue S.E. - 1886.
The eclectic Queen Anne vocabulary, with its Old English roots, gave the Gothic Revival a final spin.

timbered wall surface they nailed vertical, horizontal, and diagonal boards to the sides of ordinary wood-frame houses. The same idea had been tried out fifteen years earlier by Richard Morris Hunt on a summer home in Newport, Rhode Island.

American architects took a year or so to assimilate this new "surface style" and arrange to dash off some copies. In January 1878 the firm of George and Charles Palliser of Bridgeport, Connecticut published *Palliser's American Cottage Homes*. In the drawings, Eastlake table legs held up the porches and Jacobean chimney stacks soared over high-pitched Tudor roofs. Yet it was all remarkably American. One could not see an English manor in the outline of a balloon-frame house proportioned for an American street.

With the exception of foundations and chimneys, 35 of the 37 houses illus-

Des Moines - 2000 Grand Avenue - 1881-83. A genuine mansion with third-floor ballroom, Herndon Hall was built by Jefferson Polk, one-time law partner of Frederick Hubbell. At some point the original wooden porches were removed and the porta cochere was pulled back toward the front entrance, giving an even clearer view of the Neo-Jacobean influence that launched the Queen Anne Style. It is now an office building.

trated by the Pallisers were entirely of wood. Ground floors were covered in standard American clapboard, while second stories were usually sheathed in "fishscale" shingles that resembled tongue-shaped English wall tiles. So much extraneous wood was nailed on that some walls were divided into a veritable checkerboard of rectangles, many of which were filled with decorative panels of original design.

In our own century this architect's idiom has been called the *Stick Style*, a label coined in the 1950s by Vincent Scully, the dean of American architectural historians. Scully identified two principal criteria. One was "skeletal articulation" – the use of flat boards on the exterior of the house to simulate the half-timbered appearance. The second was a framework of straight trusses at the eaves where bargeboards belonged. Suffice it to say that very few Iowa houses made use of this repertoire. Before the Old English spinoff could get properly started, it was overtaken by the more classical Queen Anne.

Nineteenth century pattern books seldom used style names to characterize individual designs, so the public had trouble associating the terms they heard with the structures they saw being built. A person identified as T.D.G. of Carson, Iowa, wrote to *Carpentry and Building* magazine in 1880 with the following request:

"Would you be kind enough to illustrate through the column of your journal the characteristics of the "Queen Anne," "Elizabethan" and "Eastlake" styles of architecture."

The editor replied:

"It is quite impossible to say nowadays where one style begins and another ends. At present they are rather names than styles, and architects use them without any very clear idea of their meaning, in a great many cases. Any attempt at classification would, we fear, be misleading… At present our architects are so much in the habit of calling an eccentric design by any name that is likely to please the owner, that until something like a style has been developed out of all this confusion, it will be difficult to discuss intelligently the meaning of the various names in common use."

The door was now open to the free invention of architectural style. You could build whatever you wanted and call it whatever you wanted. Nameless decorative architecture was ordained.

Creston - Sumner and Montgomery Streets - c. 1887. One way to give depth to a decorative design was to attach a jig-sawed board to another wooden surface, and it was cheaper than having a workman chisel the same effect from a solid block. Though furniture stylist Charles Eastlake deplored these expedients, the results are routinely called Eastlake.

Tipton - 508 E. 4th Street - 1883. Conceived by New York architect S.B. Reed, this impressive house resembles the work of the Palliser Brothers. Square towers and divided wall surfaces appeared soon after Norman Shaw's Old English themes were showcased at the 1876 Philadelphia Exposition.

Eastlake — Gothic Redux Erroneously Named

One contemporary book suggests that Charles Eastlake took up furniture design because he had "established a new approach to architecture" and needed "a new type of furniture to go with it." That's completely wrong, but it's typical of the wild attributions that are routinely posted to Eastlake's account.

Houses designed by Richard Norman Shaw were featured in Eastlake's *History of the Gothic Revival*, but though the author had nothing whatever to do with the choice of Shaw's Old English themes, American replicas are often described as "typically" and "authentically" Eastlake.

In 1983 the National Trust for Historic Preservation published a guide called *What STYLE is it?* The book describes the familiar categories – Greek, Gothic, Italianate, Second Empire, Queen Anne, and others – but Eastlake is not mentioned.

One of the best architectural references is *A Field Guide to American Houses* by Virginia and Lee McAlester, first published in 1984. Eastlake merits only a single sentence about the use of spindles in the Queen Anne mode, which the authors hasten to add was an American invention.

The name Eastlake would not now be linked with architectural style were it not for the fact that American designers stole the writer's fame to promote their products. In 1881 a certain John Pelton published a "Design for an Eastlake Cottage." Most of the details were exactly as Holly and the Pallisers had rendered them a few years before. When Eastlake saw what was being done in his name, he proclaimed the work "extravagant and bizarre."

The author you are now reading believes that Charles Eastlake can be ascribed three roles in the development of American architecture. First, he produced drawings of furniture, a few elements of which were transposed to the design of houses. This in itself does not count for much, because thousands of ornamental designs were created by Americans during the Eastlake heyday.

Second, by disdaining curved chair arms and sofa backs, Eastlake inadvertently promoted the use of rectangular structural shapes and geometric ornament. Most Classical decorations, and many Gothic ones, were derived from nature – the acanthus sprig of ancient Greece, the flowered garland of imperial Rome, the clinging vines of medieval England. Eastlake's break with fashion seems to have opened the door for abstract decorative treatments that had no historic precedent.

Finally and most importantly, Eastlake convinced a doubtful public that

Bedford - 908 State Street. An older Italianate house was modernized with a decorative porch sometime during the Eastlake heyday.

Ft. Madison

ornament was good. Americans were beginning to stuff their living spaces with ornamented objects because most things that looked expensive could now be cheaply rendered by some kind of machine. Soon every scrap of Victorian home furnishing was decorated with something. But was it tasteful? Eastlake said it could be, and that made all the difference.

Ironically, though Eastlake fought a rear-guard action against the excesses of the mass production marketplace, his copiers took a different view. They reasoned that if a little ornament was a good thing, a great deal of ornament was even better. There was also a doctrine called the "hierarchy of decorum" which held that the amount of decoration should reflect the status of the client. Since most Americans craved status, ornament was necessary. The result was the so-called "Gingerbread Age" when even inexpensive houses were covered with a "frosting" of extraneous wooden trinkets.

Much of the decorative wood used to adorn American houses was produced in lumber milling plants on the Iowa side

Andrew - 101 E. Benton. A date stone in the wall proves that this limestone house was built in 1872. The style of the porch suggests that it was added a few years later.

Rock Rapids - 305 S. Boone Street - c. 1880s. The authors of the new decorative forms were not English architects, but anonymous designers employed by American millwork factories.

Britt - 248 1st Avenue S.W. - 1886. Though neither label is correct, the wooden decoration seen here is usually called Eastlake, while the angled bay windows and square tower (removed about 1940) are associated with the Queen Anne Style. The complexity of the design suggests that it probably came from a pattern book, but it might have been assembled by a local builder using standardized millwork products. The current color scheme is undoubtedly more challenging than the original.

---

of the Mississippi River. One mill catalog showed 132 different designs for the headblocks that were commonly used at the corners of interior door frames. The cheapest could be had for five cents a copy.

The Gothic bargeboard was now rendered not as a strip of perforated plank running the entire breadth of the gable, but as a handy-sized triangle that could be tucked into any likely corner. It would cost $1,500 to build your house, and since the jig-sawed gable end added a mere $2, why not have one? You could buy it with confidence knowing that it could be easily adjusted to fit the pitch of your roof. In fact, if you had a ladder you could nail it up yourself. It was not authentic Eastlake, but who cared?

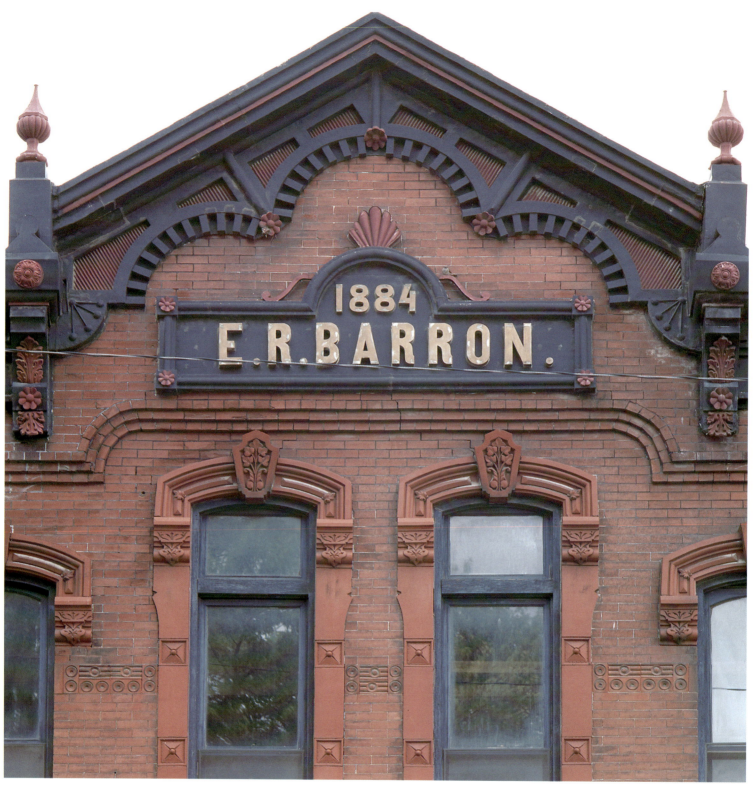

McGregor - 1884. The cornice sections and ornamental window caps were stamped from galvanized iron or steel. The two ferrous metals are differentiated by their carbon contents and smelting methods, but cannot be visually distinguished. Identical designs are found on stores in other towns.

Oskaloosa - 1885. If the date displayed is correct, this was one of the first all-metal facades. The decorative elements prove that the Italianate vocabulary was still in vogue.

Albia - 1889. The Skean's Block is Iowa's most glamourous commercial building of the Victorian period. Spanning two store entrances, the large pediment, dentiled cornice, and decorative window caps are made of galvanized metal. Stained glass above the display windows is a rare feature.

Manning. Adjoining metal window caps on light-color brick walls give this town's main street a distinctive touch.

1887

Sixty years ago an old newspaper reporter named Cyrenus Cole penned *I Remember I Remember*, one chapter of which was titled "Des Moines in the Year 1887." He recalled that the capital city's population had grown to almost 40,000, but that the streets were choked with mud when it rained and dust when it didn't. Cole called it an "overgrown village."

Court Avenue was the leading thoroughfare. A few years earlier, cheap frame shanties had earned Walnut Street, just one block north, the epithet "Rat Row." Now the shacks were being knocked down, and handsome brick buildings were taking their places. New houses of commerce were sprouting on adjoining blocks as well.

Despite the obvious signs of prosperity all around them, the city fathers were restive. It was remarked that the two tallest buildings in town rose to a height of only six stories. One of these, facing the courthouse square, belonged to Mr. Youngerman. The other was the new Savery hotel on 4th Street. Wrote Cole:

"Des Moines was then abnormally obsessed with the desire to become a bigger city. Like a boy who wants to be a man, it wanted to grow up. But at that time it was not growing."

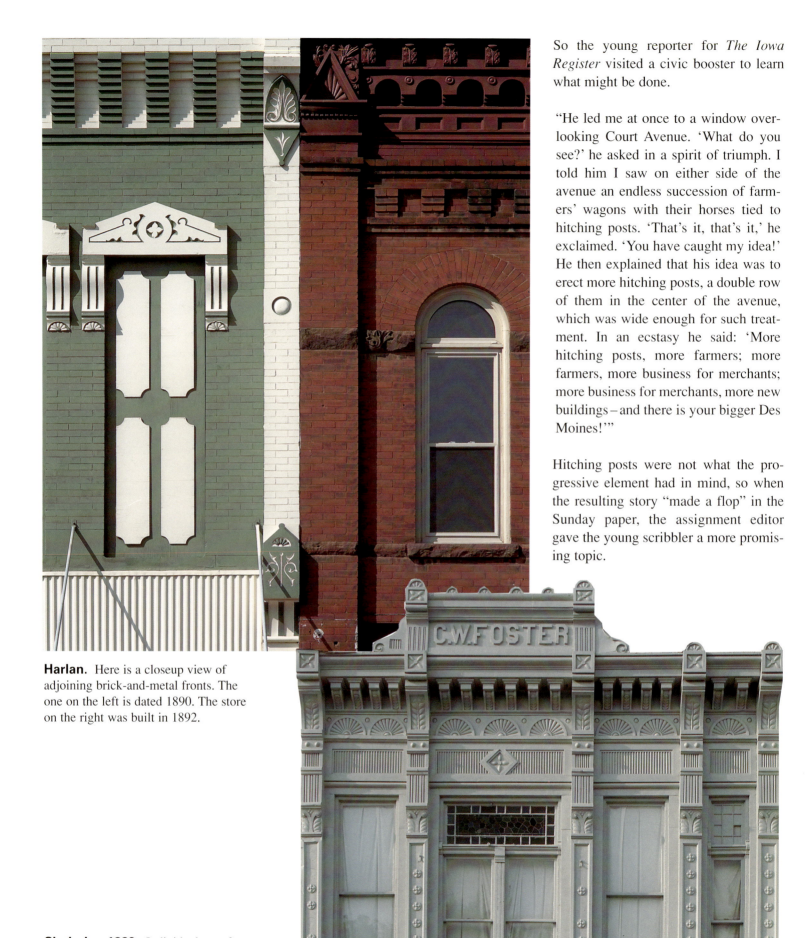

So the young reporter for *The Iowa Register* visited a civic booster to learn what might be done.

"He led me at once to a window overlooking Court Avenue. 'What do you see?' he asked in a spirit of triumph. I told him I saw on either side of the avenue an endless succession of farmers' wagons with their horses tied to hitching posts. 'That's it, that's it,' he exclaimed. 'You have caught my idea!' He then explained that his idea was to erect more hitching posts, a double row of them in the center of the avenue, which was wide enough for such treatment. In an ecstasy he said: 'More hitching posts, more farmers; more farmers, more business for merchants; more business for merchants, more new buildings – and there is your bigger Des Moines!'"

Hitching posts were not what the progressive element had in mind, so when the resulting story "made a flop" in the Sunday paper, the assignment editor gave the young scribbler a more promising topic.

Harlan. Here is a closeup view of adjoining brick-and-metal fronts. The one on the left is dated 1890. The store on the right was built in 1892.

Clarinda - 1889. Individual storefronts were commonly referred to as "blocks." According to the inscription, this example was built for C.W. Foster.

"To prove that the city was not dead, he asked me to roam about, count the new houses, and write cheerful interviews with the men who had built them – even if it were on the proceeds of mortgages. After I had done much rambling, counting, and interviewing, I told Mr. Jones that I could write much more interesting stories for the paper about the holes-in-the-wall that had been built for the sale of illicit liquors."

Iowa was officially a dry state, a fact that many blamed for the lack of economic vigor. Rashes of "porch climber" burglaries and pedestrian stickups were attributed to the fact that honest working men, to quench their honest thirsts, were obliged to frequent houses of ill fame.

"In 1887 there was one part of Des Moines that was not languishing. It was the part known as the Red Light District, a segregated area of considerable extent lying between the network of railroad tracks and the Raccoon River. The district was a village in its own right and one of its own kind."

It was the reporter's custom to visit the police station with a pocketful of nickel cigars. These blandishments were sure to loosen the tongues of laconic desk sergeants. One cheroot earned reporter Cole a rib-crushing ride in a paddy wagon as it raced to the scene of a violent altercation.

"There were broken chairs and broken bottles on the floor, and a half dazed man with blood on his face. The other men had escaped and the women were upstairs putting on more clothes than they had worn while they were down-

---

Clarinda - 1876 and later. Because it combines historic styles from different periods, this commercial building is exceptionally rare. The second floor is Italianate, but the street level is Romanesque. The remodeling was probably carried out in the 1890s.

Iowa City - 218-222 E. Washington

stairs. When I got back to the office the whole affair was worth no more than a few lines tucked away in an obscure corner of a Sunday morning Christian newspaper."

This first glimpse of the Red Light District aroused the reporter's curiosity.

"So one evening when the sun was about to go down I wended my way to it, to see rather than to be seen. There sunset was sunrise: the day began with darkness. The denizens of the place were getting ready for the orgies of the night that was falling. Musicians were trying out their squawky pianos, for vice has its own music and it is apt to be as ragged as its devotees. Painted women were beginning to exhibit themselves in upper windows…

"On the street corners of the place stood policemen with billy clubs and guns. They were there to protect the nefarious business of the place, not to interrupt it. The keepers of the houses paid licenses that entitled them to such protection. It was said that with such licenses they helped to support schools, and it was also whispered that one respectable man paid his pew rent in a fashionable church out of rents he received from buildings in the Red Light District.

"It was then an accepted belief that in every city there had to be about so much vice, and that it was better to segregate it and regulate it than to let it roam at will. Once in a while, when a more outrageous crime was committed in the district, there was a loud outcry for its suppression. But nothing ever came from such complaints or demands."

Meanwhile, civic leaders were organizing to promote the more wholesome

---

Dubuque - 1479 Central - 1890. The architect had two ideas about windows and decided to use them both. Even in the age of Free Classic invention, this liberty must have been considered daring.

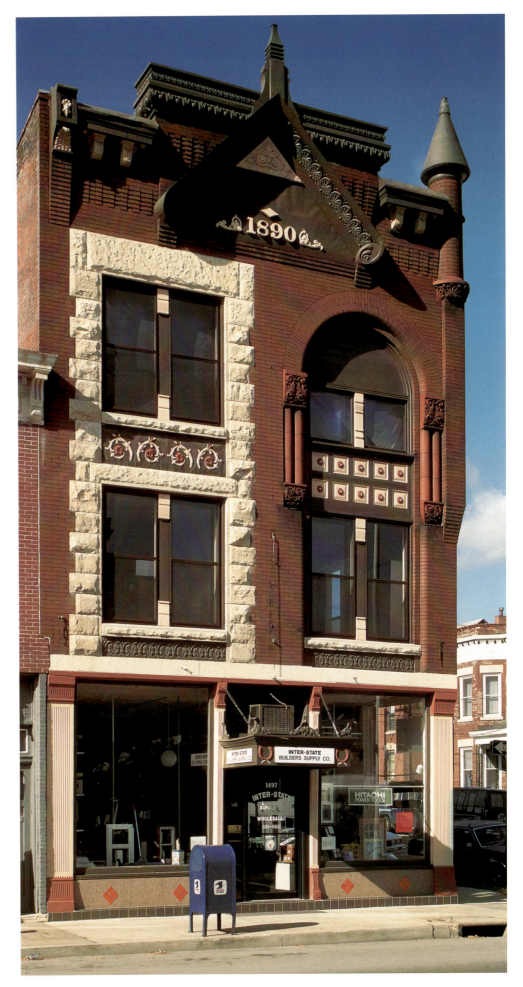

85

varieties of economic activity. In January 1888 the Commercial Exchange was created to unify separate associations. A Board of Trade had been established in 1871, followed by a Manufacturers Association in 1872. The new Exchange later became the Des Moines Chamber of Commerce. The business roster for that year listed 10 banks and 11 insurance companies.

Despite the periodic fussing about slow economic development, new commercial structures were being added to the skyline at a steady pace. In 1888, Mr. Van Ginkle completed a nine-story edifice topped with a four-story tower. The Observatory Building featured a roof garden restaurant, though reporter Cole saw little delight in the view. There was nothing much to see, he wrote, but smoke from the chimneys below.

The construction trades were busy in other quarters as well. Handsome homes climbed the side of the hill west of Hoyt Sherman's mansion, and scattered dwellings were popping up in the surrounding suburbs. In December 1888 the

Davenport - 728 Farnam Avenue - 1891. The Second Empire Style had been out of fashion for a number of years when this unusual house was built. The central tower features surprisingly large windows.

Corydon - 312 S. West Street - c. 1887. When this house was built, the Italianate brackets under the eaves were old fashioned, but the decorative porch was right in step with the latest vogue.

first electrified street car was put into service. For a nickel's fare, sightseers could now travel 12 miles of city streets. The most desirable building sites were those within easy walking distance of a car line.

The common practice was for a prospective homeowner to first purchase a vacant lot, then select a builder, but steady growth soon created a market for speculative developers. One such firm, Carpenter & Keeler Contractor-Builders, showcased its work in an 1890 newspaper ad.

"The above Cut and Floor Plans represent one of our NEW HOUSES on Sixteenth street, between Center and Crocker streets, now almost ready for occupancy. If you want to buy a well-

Des Moines - 2846 Forest Drive - c. 1892. Located in the Owl's Head Historic District, this understated design features huge windows and oversized dormers. Smooth Tuscan columns contrast with rough-finished stone in the first-floor wall. Given the size of the structure, the corner turret looks like a spinnaker billowing at the front of a ship. The vessel once belonged to Lafayette Young, newspaper publisher, state legislator, and friend of Teddy Roosevelt.

built and convenient house, with all modern improvements and in a good locality, come and see us."

By this time architects had given their full attention to the erroneously-named *Queen Anne* mode. Writing for *Harper's Magazine* in 1883, critic Montgomery Schuyler noted:

"Queen Anne is a comprehensive name which has been made to cover a multitude of incongruities, including, indeed, the bulk of recent work which otherwise defies classification, and there is a convenient vagueness about the term which fits it for that use…

"Mr. Norman Shaw has been the chief evangelist of this strange revival. Mr. Shaw is a very clever designer, with a special felicity in piquant and picturesque groupings, which he had shown in Gothic work, especially in country houses, before the caprice seized him of uniting free composition with classic detail, and the attempt at this union is what is most distinctively known as Queen Anne."

Many early Queen Anne houses looked old and English, but the label was soon taken over by American architects who gave their designs a totally unprecedented appearance. Because there was nothing like it in Europe, this new Queen Anne was the thing that everyone had been asking for – a genuinely American architecture. The leading practitioner of the new style, and the one who invented most of it, was George Franklin Barber.

Barber was born in 1854 at Dekalb, Illinois and grew up on a farm in Kansas. His early education seems to have been interrupted by the border wars, and it is now generally assumed that his knowledge of architecture was absorbed from books. By the mid 1880s he was back in Dekalb working as a residential builder. In 1888, Barber left Illinois and settled in Knoxville, Tennessee. Just prior to this move he published the *Cottage Souvenir*, a set of 18 house plans printed on punched card stock and tied together with a piece of yarn. This was apparently a form of advertising rather than a product published for sale.

The best biographical information available leaves many questions unan-

Sioux City - 1631 S. Paxton Street. The Romanesque Style features massive arches.

swered. Barber apparently hooked up with J.C. White, a real estate developer who later became his business manager. Many Barber-designed houses were built in Knoxville suburbs at about that time, and may have provided the funds for an aggressive advertising campaign. Barber was soon promoting mail-order house plans in popular magazines. A rapid increase in his business occurred in 1892 with the *Cottage Souvenir #2*, a book of 61 designs that sold for $2.00 in paperback and $2.75 in hardcover.

Barber continued to publish illustrated catalogs, and in 1895 he launched a monthly magazine called *American Homes*. Orders poured in from all over the United States and from countries as

Sioux City - 1902 Jackson - 1892. The Queen Anne tower was often thrust up from the body of the house, but here the cylinder is an integral part of the floor plan.

Grinnell - 833 East Street - 1892.
Even at the height of the style's popularity, not all Queen Anne houses were heavily ornamented. The most decorative feature of this colorful example is a set of stained glass windows.

far away as China and South Africa. By 1900 the company employed 30 draftsmen to hand-copy more than 800 designs, and 20 secretaries were kept busy answering the mail.

Several authorities have written that George Barber was the first to sell prefabricated houses in crates, but others who have researched Barber's work say there is no evidence that he was actually engaged in manufacturing. It is certainly true that manufactured windows, doors, staircases and other components were routinely shipped by rail to lumber yards and contractors, and that a number of millwork companies advertised in his magazine. What is not clear is whether entire houses were sold as kits until after 1900. Barber's own statements seem to disprove the assumption that he was involved in prefabrication.

"Knowing as I do that my working drawings, when they leave the office, go out of reach of my personal supervision, I have taken special pains to make everything plain and easily understood by mechanics generally. Every detail that goes from this office is full size and drawn by hand, not printed. Everything

Vinton - 608 E. 4th Street - c. 1890s.
Designs with divided wall surfaces were first presented to the home building public by the Palliser Brothers in 1878.

Prairie City - 200 W. Jefferson - c. 1887. The spindled porch was already well established, but the Queen Anne tower was just beginning to emerge from the roof like a butterfly from a chrysalis. The cover photo of this house was taken from a block away with a long lens. Viewed from the street in front, the grain elevator is less imposing.

requiring it has a detail given, and they are all ready to be pricked off on the material for working out."

It has been estimated that as many as 20,000 sets of plans were mailed from his office over the course of two decades.

Barber is said to have used the term *Romanesque* to characterize some of his features, especially towers and turrets. To qualify as authentically Romanesque, a building's walls had to be made of dark-red stone, or at the very least brick. One might, however, simply borrow the shape of the Romanesque tower and add it to the Queen Anne vocabulary, and this is apparently what Barber did. It must be noted, however, that the Richardsonian Romanesque style was already well established when Barber began his work, and if he could borrow a prominent design feature, so could others. One can undoubtedly find towered Queen Annes dated prior to Barber's first use of this element.

The Queen Anne and Romanesque styles did not have the field entirely to themselves. In 1887 the Palliser brothers were back in the book stalls with *New Cottage Homes*.

"It would be folly for us who live in

Eldora - 15th and Washington. The Classical influence is evident in the window treatment of this typical Queen Anne house of the 1890s.

the nineteenth century, in a nation noted for its inventive genius, to undertake to transplant to this new country any foreign style which was perfected centuries ago. Instead, there is springing up a National style which is becoming more distinctive in character, and unlike that of any other nation."

Never mind that the Pallisers had been deeply involved in the "folly" of previous transplants, their new mode – "Old Colonial" – was indeed closer to home. A house in this style was a side-gabled box with a small entry porch and perfectly symmetrical window placement. If you didn't like the assertive Queen Anne look, here was the obvious antithesis.

A modest revival of early-American forms began about 1883 when the New York firm of McKim, Mead, and White built a few spacious houses that looked passably Colonial. Neither these nor the Pallisers' contributions earned many adherents, however. The Queen Anne was far too popular.

Dubuque - Grove Terrace - 1890. Here is a rare Gothic Survival. New styles appeared in rapid succession, but some folks preferred a traditional look.

OPPOSITE
Sioux City - 1721 Rebecca Street - c. 1885-89. Despite the relatively narrow front, the Romanesque Style never looked more imposing. A spooky medieval turret is balanced by a friendly porch with cheery trim so that the overall effect is mysteriously inviting.

Dubuque - Grove Terrace - c. 1891. Now a bed-and-breakfast, this large Queen Anne house clings to the side of a hill overlooking the business district.

Romanesque *Ancient Stones Speak Again*

Romanesque architecture is even older than the Gothic. By the year 800 the emperor Charlemagne had conquered most of continental Europe. His favorite castle, completed in 794, combined elements of Byzantine architecture with the surviving Roman influences of northern Italy. In the reigns of his successors, great blocks of stone were quarried to build churches and monasteries. Roman barrel vaulting and massive half-circle arches were the primary visual features.

In 19th century America, Romanesque precedent was employed in the design of churches and other large structures from the 1840s on. Its complete revival, however, was the work of one man – Henry Hobson Richardson. Born to a prosperous Louisiana family, he graduated from Harvard in 1859 and

Sioux City - 2901 Jackson Street - 1891-94. Constructed over a period of three years, this weighty structure is a superb example of Richardsonian Romanesque. The first owner lost his fortune in the Crash of '93, raffled the house in 1900, and moved to Seattle. It is now the Sioux City Public Museum.

promptly sailed for Paris to enroll at the famed school of architecture, the Ecole des Beaux Arts. The only American to precede him there was Richard Morris Hunt who went on to design mansions for the Vanderbilts. The first architectural college in America – at MIT – was not founded until 1866.

After an apprenticeship in the firm of a noted French architect, Richardson arrived in New York in 1865, opened a small office, and began entering architectural competitions. Though fully versed in the Classical idiom, he had his heart set on something else – the ancient forms of the middle ages. Increasingly important commissions culminated in 1877 with the completion of Boston's Trinity Church, still regarded as one of America's finest buildings. Universal acclaim was instantaneous, and the 39-year-old Richardson was showered with commissions for libraries, court houses, city halls, banks, and railroad stations.

At the height of his fame, and with an army of disciples enrolled in his cause, Richardson died in 1886. With the master's light extinguished, the flourishing style began a slow departure and by the turn of the century it was gone.

Because it sought to achieve beauty through strength, the style depended upon massive forms and expensive materials. Romanesque required high roofs, clustered windows, deeply arched doorways, and protruding towers. One doubter remarked that it was "defensible only in military terms," so it is not surprising that relatively few houses were executed in the style. Its monumental proportions were best suited to commercial buildings.

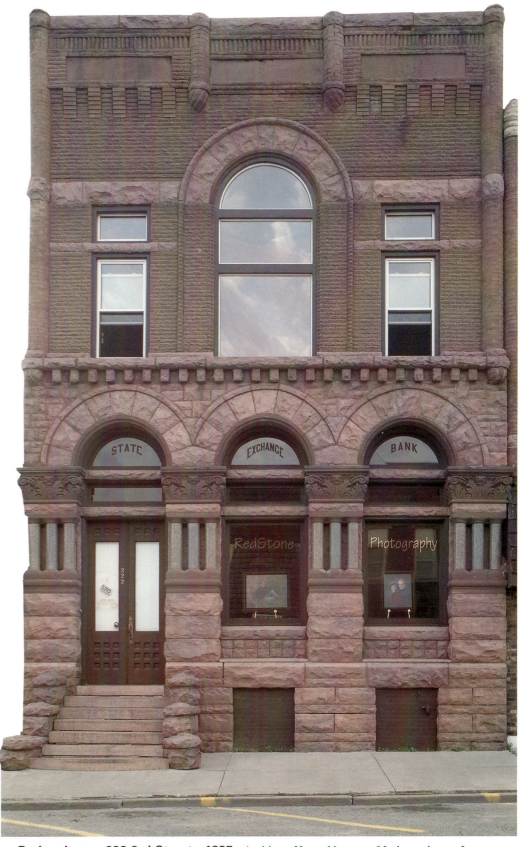

Parkersburg - 222 3rd Street - 1895. Architect Harry Netcott of Independence, Iowa, was obviously familiar with the work of H.H. Richardson. This late version of the Romanesque was originally a bank.

Osceola - 502 S. Main Street - 1892. In this version of the Queen Anne, geometric effects are substituted for the usual Classical decorations. It has half-circle window openings in the twin front gables, a small balcony where one can inhale the morning air, and a porch that unbalances the composition.

Council Bluffs - 126 Park Avenue - 1890. Twin front gables and an angled bay window typify the unrestrained character of Norman Shaw's Free Classic idiom.

Queen Anne *Freeform Composition with Classical Detail*

By 1887 the *Free Classic* style of Richard Norman Shaw was beginning to evolve a new set of forms. Commercial buildings and blocks of flats in major cities hewed closest to the Queen Anne prototype – Shaw's New Zealand Chambers of 1872. But the kind of house we now call Queen Anne was a genuinely American invention.

Architects took full advantage of balloon frame construction to expand the house in every direction. A bay window might jut out from a load-bearing wall only to be superseded by a pedimented gable that loomed out even farther. To puncture the envelope and unbalance the composition, a square bay was sometimes cut into a corner at an angle of 45 degrees. And though no Englishman of Queen Anne's reign ever lounged on a wrap-around porch, the sprawling American veranda was now a dominant feature. The only rule of proportion was that there were no rules of proportion.

Complicated roof planes were a hallmark of the English manor house, so Queen Anne roofs often had gables pointing in several directions. However, within the relatively small footprint of an American house, gabling opportunities were often limited. To overcome this, architects placed gables one in front of another, with the forward triangle at a slightly lower elevation and offset to one side. It was a shingle layer's nightmare, but the effect was striking.

Fairfield - 401 E. Burlington - 1896.
This house was built from one of George Barber's most popular plans. It's like a giant layer cake, with a different point of emphasis on every level.

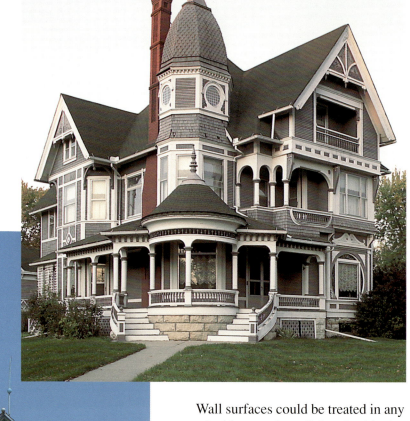

Wall surfaces could be treated in any conceivable way, from fishscale shingles and latticed stick patterns to classical swags and geometrical sunbursts. Fan shaped windows that once topped the entry doors of Federal Style houses were now greatly enlarged and set into gables. Little second-story balconies were either tucked into the walls or thrust boldly forward as overhanging projections.

The decorative Queen Anne vocabulary emphasized the Classical, so one might expect to see garlands, columns, and carved wood that resembled plaster pargetting. Medieval influences were not entirely forgotten, so if your taste ran to Gothic you could choose a triangular wooden gable end perforated with jig-sawed ornament. Rows of purely American stick-and-ball porch spindles were popular, but so were carved brackets of vaguely Italian origin. The great delight of the Queen Anne mode was that almost

Grundy Center - 1002 7th Street.
"Painted Lady" color schemes are modern reflections of authentic decor. Vibrant colors were commonly used to highlight decorative features.

Mount Vernon - 725 1st Street W. - 1892.
A bulky rectangular elevation substitutes for the round Queen Anne tower.

Vinton - 913 2nd Avenue - c. 1892.
This impressive house demonstrates the varied textures of the popular "surface style." It is now a bed-and-breakfast.

anything could be fitted under its expansive umbrella.

Of all the features that distinguish the Queen Anne Style, the most easily recognized is the tower, a cylindrical or polygonal structure topped with a conical "candle snuffer." If a tower materializes from a wall without touching the ground, it's called a turret. This feature was not one of Norman Shaw's legacies, so its precise origin is something of a mystery.

Some Queen Anne houses have the tower situated at the junction of two wings in exactly the same position as the tower of the Italian Villa. The shapes are different, but the massings are remarkably similar. Given the spirit of Free Classic invention, it is no great leap to suppose that a free-thinking designer simply leaked a bit of the Italianate into the Queen Anne. Still, it was probably H.H. Richardson's Romanesque influence that got the job done.

Forest City - 345 N. Clark. This attractive Queen Anne wears a sparkling necklace of decorative porch details.

Des Moines - 753 19th Street - c. 1880. The porch trim – typical of the mass-produced millwork of the period – is thought to have been added in the 1890s.

Red Oak - 711 E. Coolbaugh - 1893. This is one of Iowa's most elegant historic homes. The fenestration of the gable resembles a Palladian window, but the opening is equipped with small Tuscan columns and a band of Classical festoons. The lone dormer is equally unusual – a half-circle opening topped with a Classical pediment. The front steps are guarded by rampant lions that seem right at home.

Bloomfield - 1893. This county-seat town owns one of the state's finest collections of iron-front stores.

1894

Learning that Kelly's Army had pushed off from Van Meter in Dallas County at about nine o'clock Saturday night, officials deployed a force of 75 policemen and deputy sheriffs at 1:30 Sunday morning. It was noon, however, before the first "California Industrials" wandered into the Valley Junction rail yard. Caught in a drenching rain storm, the "army" had scattered to take shelter for the night in haystacks and roadside barns. In the morning they struggled on with soggy blankets over their shoulders and empty dinner pails in their hands. Herded by police into a field west of Walnut Creek, the 1,400 destitute men in tattered clothes made a dismal spectacle. Many had no shoes.

When Charles Kelly, leader of the expedition, arrived on the scene, he demanded a thousand loaves of bread, a thousand pounds of beef, and fifty pounds of coffee. In anticipation of their coming, supplies had been collected at the Commercial Exchange in Des Moines, but Mayor Hillis had directed that all provisions be delivered to the old stove works on the east side. The "commonwealers" had rolled into Omaha aboard a stolen Union Pacific train and had been temporarily detained by the National Guard. There was no telling what this mob of ruffians might do. The mayor did not want the army fed until it had passed peacefully through the center of the city.

Members of "the citizens committee" disregarded the mayor's instructions and drove west on Grand Avenue with several wagon loads of supplies. As they neared the Walnut Creek bridge, police seized the bridles and told James Baird Weaver he could not proceed. The

Jefferson. Identical elements can be seen in Harlan, Oakland, Columbus Junction, and other Iowa towns.

Traer - 1894. The spiral staircase attached to the Star Clipper newspaper office is responsible for the slogan "Wind Up In Traer."

Washington

indignant 61-year old politician challenged the officers to arrest him. When they hesitated he whipped up the horses and ran the gantlet.

The police were understandably wary of the bombastic Weaver. In 1880 the Congressman from Iowa had been nominated for the Presidency by the Greenback-Labor Party and had polled more than 300,000 votes. The original Greenback Party was organized after the economic collapse of 1873. Its followers believed that the mass printing of inflationary paper money would ease the burdens of debt-ridden farmers. By 1878 an urban constituency had been added to the coalition.

Though the Greenbackers at one time held 14 seats in Congress, the party dissolved after a poor showing in the 1884 elections. In 1891, with hard times again looming on the economic horizon, the Populist Party was formed at a convention in Cincinnati and Weaver, a noted Civil War general, was again chosen as the standard bearer. In the 1892 presidential election he garnered more than a million ballots and 22 electoral votes.

New Hampton - Main and Locust. When the Queen Anne Style was adapted to commercial buildings, turrets and bay windows were often suspended over the sidewalk. Coverings of galvanized sheet iron were embossed with Classical swags and other Renaissance ornaments.

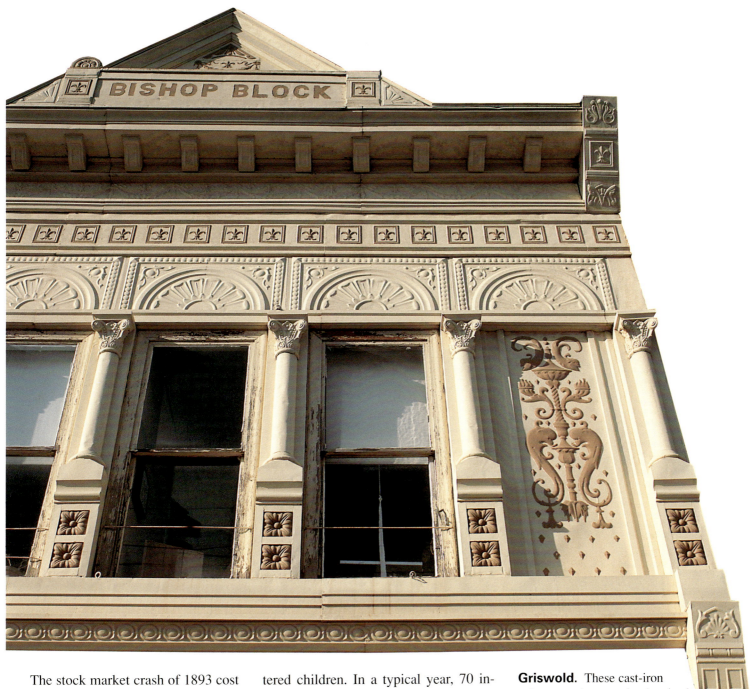

Griswold. These cast-iron columns and stamped galvanized panels were probably produced in one of the Mesker Brothers' factories and shipped to the site with a set of numbered instructions.

The stock market crash of 1893 cost thousands their livelihoods. There had been other financial panics, but this proved to be the most devastating collapse in nearly sixty years. To many it seemed that the nation was coming apart. There was talk of revolution in the air, and several state governors called out militias to put down labor riots. Even before the crash, conditions in America's largest cities had become intolerable. Women labored in sweat shops while unemployed men idled on the steps of filthy tenements. Crime exploded at six times the rate of population growth, and aid societies rescued thousands of battered children. In a typical year, 70 infants were found dead in the streets of New York.

Missionaries of every stripe found audiences increasingly receptive to radical preachings. Iowa College, later Grinnell College, was the capital of Christian Socialism, and Professor George Herron was its prophet. The college chapel was the only room on campus large enough for his lectures, and his big-city appearances drew crowds of thousands. Herron spoke of America's "stupid national conceit" and "the wicked moral blindness of our industrialism."

Hampton - 103 2nd Avenue S.E. - c. 1895. The roof is fitted with decorative false gables. The bay window, filled with a single piece of curved glass, is an unusual feature. Ten colors were used to accentuate the design.

"This social strain, this winter of unemployment and want, is without excuse to a righteous reason. There is no war, no pestilence, no failure of harvests. There is an abundance in our land for the people. Yet this richest nation of the world, in the midst of a material prosperity so marvelous as to become the object of political worship, suddenly finds a vast population face to face with famine."

While Herron laid the moral groundwork for an undoing of power, others were preparing to vote with their feet. Early in 1894 a populist named Jacob Coxey organized the unemployed of Ohio for a march on Washington. His

Maquoketa - 209 E. Locust - c. 1895. Most Queen Anne houses are large, and this is no exception. The volumes were calculated to give plenty of living space to bustling households.

Fort Madison - 903 Avenue E - 1896. The body of the house is markedly Romanesque, but the roofline features an Elizabethan gable.

announced goal was a massive public works program to be funded with interest-free bonds and $500 million in new paper money. Others followed his example and soon a dozen armies of impoverished malcontents were on the move, each headed by a self-appointed "general." As General Kelly was marching toward Des Moines, General Fry was passing through Indianapolis and General Galvin's men were massing near Pittsburgh.

Among the most daring "Coxeyites" were Sander's Cripple Creek Industrials, who stole a train at Pueblo, Colorado and made a dash for the east. When an engine was overturned on the tracks to block them, the resourceful miners, accustomed to working with picks and shovels, tore up a hundred feet of track behind them, laid the rails past the obstruction, and sped into Kansas with federal marshalls in hot pursuit.

Meanwhile, on the west side of the bridge over Walnut Creek, it was now 5:30 on the afternoon of April 30, 1894. With his army fed, General Kelly mounted a big bay horse and got the men to their feet.

"I tell you we are going to Washington. We are going in spite of all the forces

Parkersburg - 401 5th Street - 1895. A wrap-around wooden porch is gone, but the surprising alteration concerns the arched entrance. In old photographs it is a second-story walkout and there is another brick porch below it. It appears that for some reason the ground-level structure was removed and the top layer was lowered to take its place. If that is what happened, how it was accomplished in the 1920s is anyone's guess. The result is a difference in the color of the brick wall on two sides of a ragged line.

that may oppose us, to ask for a chance to earn a living. We are going to urge Congress to give employment to those who can't get it otherwise. We did not bid our little ones goodbye to falter now."

And so the march resumed. *The Daily Iowa Capital* reported:

"They were gotten in line and started for the city… the long column of footsore, discouraged and homeless wanderers on a vague and seemingly purposeless mission to the fat-witted Democratic president at Washington… Their arrival had been anticipated and the downtown streets were lined by thousands of curious people."

When the army was finally bedded down at the stove works, the mayor breathed a sigh of relief.

The following day, as efforts were underway to feed the unwelcome visitors, newspaper reporters were scurrying for angles. Said the *Capital*:

"Sheriff McGarraugh, when asked if

Tipton - 104 E. 7th Street - 1898. Colonial elements include a Palladian window in the third-floor gable and a scrolled pediment over the porch. Though not forgotten, the tower is beginning to lose its importance.

St. Ansgar - 513 W. 4th Street - 1896. When he received his plans by mail from George Barber's office in Knoxville, Tennessee, the client chose to leave off some of the ornamental features. The blueprints called for lathe-turned porch posts and connecting spindles, but the builder chose Tuscan columns instead. When the house became a bed-and-breakfast in 1992, the renovators added Italianate brackets salvaged from another house. An original gable decoration is still missing.

what was later described as a police riot, officers waded into the mob with clubs flying. Fifty men were trampled or bludgeoned as Coxey tumbled over a wall and disappeared in the shrubbery. Mounted officers leapt their horses over the wall and chased Coxey down as he sprinted toward the Capitol steps. He was arrested for walking on the lawn.

Back in Des Moines, word was circulated that Kelly would deliver an address that evening at the Trades Assembly Hall. When the hour arrived, the streets around the building were packed with people trying to get inside, so the gathering was moved to the east front of the Polk County Courthouse.

Said the *Capital*:

"For about forty minutes in a voice that vibrated with well simulated emotion, Kelly held the immense crowd, the unwieldy size of which made it impossible to hear his remarks on the

he had any intention of employing force to compel the army to leave town, replied that he did not; that he did not believe that he had any right to employ force so long as the men observed the law. 'Then, again,' said Joe, as a dubious look mounted his face, 'what the dickens would I do if they refused to go? If I should arrest the army I would be compelled to feed every man in it three square meals a day. Then where could I put them if I had them?'"

Meanwhile in the nation's capital, General Coxey, vanguard of the "living petition to Congress," rode in a carriage at the head of a ragged procession. Down Pennsylvania Avenue the route was unobstructed, but at the foot of the Capitol the way was barred. Thirty thousand onlookers stared at 500 marchers and waited to see what would happen. In

Dubuque - 1337 Main Street. This example began life as a twin-towered Queen Anne, but gained a pediment and a colonnade of Neo-Classical columns about ten years later. You will not see another one like it.

Keokuk - 816 Grand Street - c. 1897. This expensive Queen Anne house is one of the few made of stone and brick. Now a bed-and-breakfast, it overlooks the Mississippi River.

Vinton - 1303 A Avenue - 1901. Paired Tuscan columns were a popular porch treatment at the turn of the century.

Perry - 1716 Willis Avenue - 1898. The entrance is set at a 45-degree angle, with Gothic gable ends above and Classical columns below.

pects of transportation save their sturdy legs, the army was reduced Sunday to the necessity of devising some means of getting out of town. In this dilemma Kelly's attention was called to the possibility of making the journey to Keokuk by water… Having been assured the assistance of the Carpenter's union in building boats and a plentiful supply of food while the work was in progress, Kelly went to Gilcrist's lumber yard early Sunday morning, planked down $507 and ordered lumber for 150 flat boats."

There was no report as to how Kelly had come by these funds, but no one really

outer edges… The adroitness and consummate diplomacy of the man in arousing sympathy by assuming a highly religious tone and bearing, in opening his meetings with the well known hymn, 'Nearer My God to Thee,' and closing them with the doxology, is rapidly driving the detectives to a life of dissipation… He has a really fine choir of male voices, and when they sing 'Where Is My Wandering Boy Tonight' Kelly weeps pathetically and nearly every woman within hearing weeps with him. He worked this lay very cleverly last evening."

In the days that followed, Kelly's troops maintained proper decorum and no crimes were reported. To pass the time the army got up a baseball team and lost a game to a local outfit. Patience, however, was wearing thin, and the flow of private charity was dwindling. The $7,000 it would take to export the army by train could not be found.

On Monday, May 7th, the *Capital* ran the headline: "TO FLOAT IN BOATS."

"Having little or no food and no pros-

cared. The army was going.

"In less than an hour a dozen teams were at work hauling lumber to the point just south of Coon River where it flows into the Des Moines, which Kelly had selected as the favored spot upon which to establish a navy yard."

Police put up ropes to keep spectators back as the men began to wield hammers and saws. The so-called boats were crude barges sixteen feet long and seven feet wide, with a foot of lumber on the sides to keep out the water. Made of one-inch pine planks nailed together, they were chinked with cotton and hemp and liberally splattered with paving tar. It was hoped that these craft would prove worthy of the 265 river miles to Keokuk. Weighing about 400 pounds, they could be easily portaged around dams by the ten passengers each was expected to carry.

On May 9th the *Capital* announced "A GAY DEPARTURE." An estimated 15,000 people swarmed the river banks to watch the army, now navy, take to the water.

"The cheers of the thousands on the shores were taken up and answered from the fleet moving down the river. It was a sight such as made the blood mantle the cheeks and tingle in the veins of all who saw it. Almost without exception the boats were gaily decorated with bunting, flags, streamers and white banners."

Someone on shore was given the job of counting the navy as it departed. The newspaper reported that 1,337 had floated away. About a hundred men stayed behind in the city, but a like number of local residents were reported to have taken their places. The newspaper guessed that "fully 500 women" were taken aboard. Most intended to jump ashore a few miles downstream, but there was at least one disgruntled husband who muttered about the more than temporary loss of his wife. One of the

Villisca - 113 N. 5th Street - 1897. This Queen Anne house employed a variety of period ornaments. Geometric gable ends cast shadows on fishscale shingles, stick-and-ball curtains spanned interior doorways, and the front entrance was adorned with a stained glass window. Despite all this luxury, there was no indoor plumbing. The original candle snuffer was removed when the porch was replaced about 1920. Though the design is attributed to a local builder, the circular "moongate" effect in the front wall was probably copied from a George Barber catalog.

boats capsized in view of the bridges, flinging women into the water. Though they were quickly rescued, the sight apparently dissuaded others from taking the risk. Afterward only men were seen shoving off.

In those days an amazing, unexpected occurrence was called "A Nine Days' Wonder." So it was fitting that Kelly's coming and going had commanded precisely nine days of newsprint. Even as the army was preparing to depart, the papers announced the next spectacle. Midway Plaisance – "The Famous World's Fair Street" – would be "reproduced in all its former attractiveness and splendor." To the citizens of Des Moines, remote from the grimmest scenes of the nation's unrest, it scarcely mattered that 300,000 coal miners were out on strike. The Midway was coming.

Midway Plaisance, namesake of all subsequent midways, was a mile-long avenue of amusements on the grounds of the 1893 Chicago world's fair. Many of the displays were theatrical stage sets of distant locales, populated with actors made up to resemble native inhabitants. When the fair closed, some of the scenery was packaged and sent on tour. The Des Moines appearance, which opened on May 14th, was described by the *Register*.

"The parade in the afternoon was very fine and certainly one of the most brilliant pageants that has ever been seen in the state. The Knights of Pythias rode on horseback followed by a squad of Columbian Guards, then came Indians, Laplanders, Samoans, and representatives of the great tribes of the world… The women of the different tribes followed in carriages and completed a long line… The doors

Davenport - 204 Prospect Avenue - 1896. Because the dust had barely settled on the 1893 Columbian Exposition, you will not find a Neo-Classical mansion built much earlier than this one. An open balcony inside the portico has been enclosed.

opened at the Tabernacle at 7:30 and from then on till the closing hour there was a throng constantly coming and going."

The Calvary Tabernacle was a non-sectarian mission located in the 400 block of East Grand. To house even a portion of the Midway Plaisance, it must have been a spacious hall. There were references in the press to the appearance outside of "captive balloons" and a "Ferris Wheel." If there was a Ferris Wheel it was certainly not the one from Chicago. The world's fair wheel, erected by Pittsburgh bridge builder George Ferris, rose to a height of 264 feet. Each of the 36 cars held 60 people, 40 of whom could be seated on plush-covered swivel chairs.

The World's Columbian Exposition was planned to commemorate the 400th anniversary of Columbus' voyage of discovery. Chicago had just reached a population of one million by annexing 120 square miles of suburbs. It lobbied so hard for the privilege of hosting the fair that the *New York Sun* dubbed Chicago the "windy city" for the "hot air" emanating from its boosters. In 1889 a group of promoters floated $5 million in bonds to get the show going, and in 1890 Congress gave its approval. In the end, the task of mounting the fair on schedule proved too much even for Chicago, and it opened a year late.

The firm of Burnham and Root was chosen to oversee the architecture. In 1886 they produced Chicago's Rookery, one of the first steel-frame office blocks. To design the principal structures they called in famous architects, muralists, and decorators from all over the country. After one planning session at a Chicago restaurant, the eminent sculptor Augustus Saint-Gaudens proclaimed it "the greatest meeting of artistic minds since the Renaissance."

Henry Van Brunt of Kansas City was the most persuasive spokesman for "the new academic style" based on the ancient Greek and Roman orders. Thirty-eight states and 19 foreign coun-

Carroll - 705 N. Carroll Street - 1903. The Neo-Classical style was not the last revival of ancient precedent. Collegiate Gothic and Stockbroker Tudor were popular in the 1920s.

Red Oak - 1020 Boundary - 1897. The Neo-Classical style is sometimes erroneously called Colonial Revival. The American antecedent is actually the Greek Revival of the 1830s.

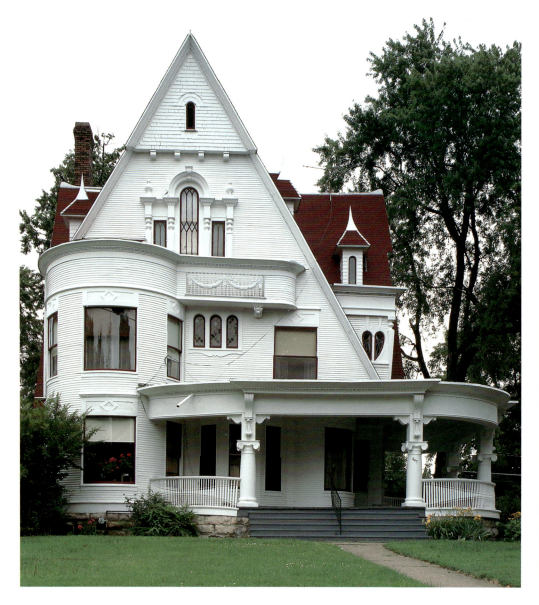

Marshalltown - 607 Main Street - 1902. Here is an eclectic composition that defies classification. There is a bit of the Queen Anne in the bulging two-story cylinder, a touch of the Neo-Classical in the stubby Ionic porch columns, and a hint of Colonial Revival in the third-floor Palladian window. With all that, the plunging slope of the gable seems to have been borrowed from the French Chateauesque. A genuinely odd design, it is also one of the most satisfying.

tries could choose their own styles of architecture, he said, but each of the ten exhibit halls should be fronted with a soaring colonnade of Classical columns.

In July 1891 construction began in Jackson Park on 633 acres that had been deemed unsuitable for commercial development. Located on Chicago's southern lake shore between 55th and 67th Streets, it was a marshy flat covered with reeds and scrub vegetation. To help finance the audacious undertaking, the U.S. Treasury struck 2.5 million commemorative half dollars.

The underlying structures were sheds made of timber and steel, but decorative exteriors were molded from an ocean of "staff" – a lightweight but reasonably durable mixture of plaster, cement, and jute fiber. To cover vast surfaces in a short time, compressed-air "squirt guns" would be used to drench the buildings in paint. As soon as the die was cast in favor of Classical ornament, the noted painter Francis Millet, Director of Decoration, announced that if only one color could be used, it had to be white. On opening day, May 1, 1893, Chicago banned the burning of coal so that the "White City" could remain white.

The stock market crashed soon after the exposition opened, but impending doom did not keep tourists from spending fifty cents to view the most lavish display of architectural splendor the world had ever seen. Commanding the Court of Honor was George Post's enormous Manufacturing and Liberal Arts Building, with a footprint covering 1.3 million square feet. In six months the White City's turnstiles recorded the passing of 27.5 million people, thousands of whom were from Iowa.

In May 1894 dust swirled in the White City's empty streets as the trappings of Midway Plaisance were exhibited in Des Moines. On May 19th, the day the show closed, Kelly's Navy was reported to have landed below Keokuk with about two-thirds of its barges intact. They were eventually towed by a steamboat part way up the Ohio River, but along the Indiana and Kentucky shores the men deserted in droves. General Kelly, minus his troops, reached Washington in July. On July 5th the White City's deserted Court of Honor went up in flames. Arson was suspected.

In *The Story of Architecture in*

Villisca - 112 3rd Street - 1902. The body of the house displays a Colonial influence, but the porch is characteristic of the fading Queen Anne.

America, Thomas Tallmadge explained why, at the end of the Victorian era, the recycling of ancient architecture was drawing its last breath.

"The arguments for an American style seem cogent and reasonable… Here we are in a new country, favored physically as is no other country in the world; we live under the aegis of a most enlightened and beneficent democracy; our culture has been signalized by great and original discoveries in the sciences and in the mechanical arts; we stand as a nation for ideals of altruism and non-aggression that were unheard-of in the chancelleries of Europe until we practised them; the sun has never shone on a nation so abundantly blessed in material prosperity. Why, then, in Heaven's name, should we go to ancient Greece and Rome, extinct for two thousand years? Why should we go to mediaeval France or Renaissance Italy or modern Europe, whose policies we condemn and whose culture we think we excel, for our architectural styles and motives?… Why should the architects alone be reactionaries? Why should they alone wear the shackles of the past when all the world walks free?"

There really is no satisfactory answer. Some have theorized that Americans built bastions of borrowed culture to ward off the advances of the machine age and preserve something recognizably safe in a landscape of rapid change. Others have guessed that the young land of America simply had to try everything

Atlantic - 103 W. 14th Street - c. 1907. A design did not have to be entirely Classical nor perfectly Colonial. This look typifies the merger of the two popular choices.

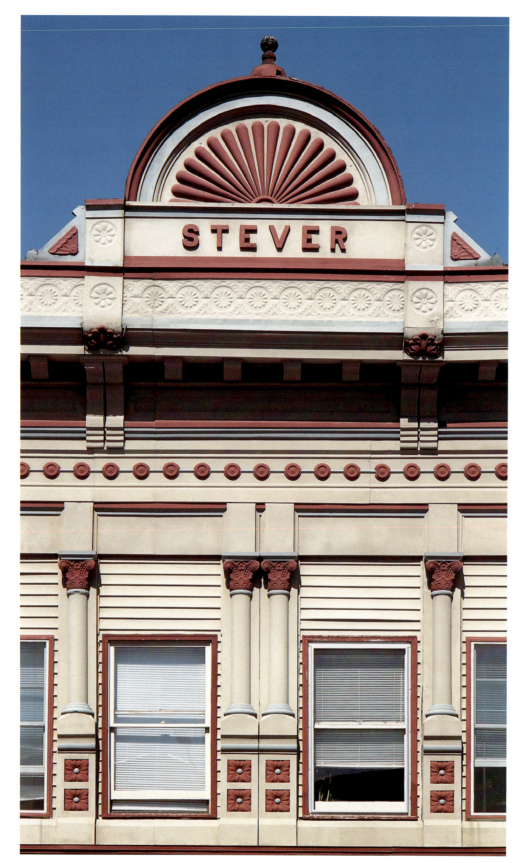

torian period so remarkable is that ten major architectural styles flourished in a span of sixty years, and that within each of the categories there were countless variations. Never before, and never since, have so many architectural forms found adherents. By comparison, today's cookie-cutter architecture is exceptionally uninspired. It is the mind-numbing repetition of modern design that makes 19th century architecture so appealing.

In the final analysis we must give the Victorians their due. They displayed a truly astonishing capacity for change, evidenced by the rapid adoption of the new and novel. The speed with which they discarded one set of models and latched onto another is proof of a rapidly evolving culture that valued spontaneity and personal expression. If anything, the Victorian architects were more inventive than those of our century.

Fairfield. When treated to a set of bright colors, decorative iron fronts spring to life.

old at least once. It should be remembered, however, that America was not alone. European culture was also locked in a perpetual time loop. It took luminaries like Frank Lloyd Wright and the European inventors of the Art Deco movement to finally cast off the bonds of architectural tradition.

The idea that the Victorians were reactionaries is not entirely correct, because invention is not the only measure of inventiveness. What makes the Vic-

Galvanized Classical *The Fully Costumed Storefront*

To the curious architectural historian, the metal-clad American storefront is still a mystery. No one has yet done the primary research necessary to explain the development of this decorative architecture, and the lack of reference material leaves secondary researchers with only a few tomes to peruse. The handful of manufacturer's catalogs that survive do not help to establish when particular components were first marketed, or who designed them.

The architectural elements in the accompanying photographs show up again and again on the storefronts of Iowa's town squares. One example displays the message "Established 1883," but this is almost certainly the year when the business was founded, not the date of the facade. Metal storefronts were advertised by their manufacturers as an inexpensive way to modernize the appearance of older buildings. Dating is further complicated by the fact that once the molds and forms were made, manufacturers continued producing the same elements for a number of years.

The storefronts shown in this chapter differ from earlier galvanized fronts in that the supporting walls are completely covered with panels and columns. Most stores of the 1870s and 1880s relied on individual elements – separate cornices and window caps – rather than integrated systems. A few of these later examples can be reliably dated to the mid 1890s.

Mechanicsville. The pilasters – rectangular engaged columns – are not exactly the same as those known to have come from the Mesker Brothers factories. Was this design produced by a competitor?

Bonaparte - 1894. Because this handsome three-story opera house was constructed soon after a fire leveled the block, it is one of the few sheet-metal facades that can be reliably dated. The multi-color paint scheme highlights the embossed details.

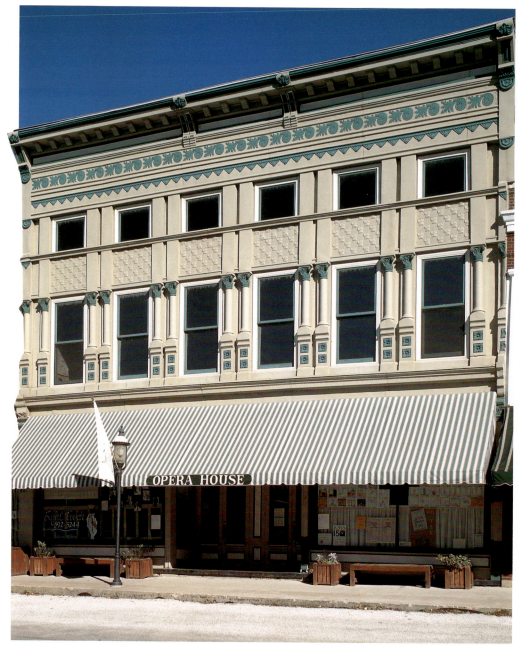

The largest firm in the business was started by the three sons of a Cincinnati tinsmith named Mesker. The first factory was at Evansville, Indiana, but two of the brothers moved on to St. Louis and set up a competing plant. Together they shipped more than 5,000 storefronts by rail – one source estimates 12,000 – each with a set of numbered instructions. Everything needed for a complete facade, including doors and windows, could be ordered in a single package. Individual pieces were riveted, soldered, and bolted together over wooden framing. Ground floors were usually equipped with load-bearing cast-iron columns, but second-floor panels were made of zinc-coated sheet steel.

Understandably, professional designers did not care for this mass-produced architecture. But legions of eager store owners were happy to avail themselves of a simple, affordable way to decorate a business block. In 1899 the price of a typical 25-foot second-story facade was $224.

Clarksville - c. 1890s. There are no other galvanized storefronts in Iowa quite like this one. The original windows were much larger than those now in use.

Forest City - 336 N. Clark Street - 1900. This impressive Neo-Classical home was designed by the Chicago firm of Beauley and Peabody. In 1945 it became a hotel, with six upstairs bedrooms renting for $2.25 a night. The Winnebago Historical Society acquired it in the 1970s.

Neo-Classical *Columns Again, and Buckets of White Paint*

With so many white-washed columns to be seen at the 1893 Columbian Exposition, and so many to see them, it was certain that the new academic style of architecture would soon command the nation's home builders. It took a few years to arrest the momentum of the fashionable Queen Anne mode and weather the effects of the deepening depression. By the late 1890s, the last years of Victoria's reign, the house-plan sellers were ready to challenge the market with fresh designs in the *Neo-Classical Style*.

Chicago's White City, the proximate cause of the new fad, got some help from abroad. The Ecole des Beaux Arts, the famous Parisian school of architecture, would admit to no style but the Classical. Young men from America went over to study and came home infected, their heads stuffed with antiquarian precedents. The monumental *Beaux Arts Style* was soon adopted for most public buildings, including Des Moines' Polk County Courthouse. By 1906 the old 1858 courthouse had been pulled down and replaced with an elegant essay in Classical Baroque. Old postcards show the roof lined with heroic statues that were never installed.

The Neo-Classical style is often mistakenly called Colonial Revival. This

Iowa Falls - 1899. The 800-seat Metropolitan Opera House was built by a local banker named Ellsworth. It opened on December 27, 1899 with Tim Murphy starring in *The Carpetbagger*, a dramatic play about a corrupt southern politician. Many of the best road companies stopped here to perform *Julius Caesar, The Prisoner of Zenda, Mrs. Wiggins in the Cabbage Patch, The Eternal City, Way Down East,* and *The Merchant of Venice,* to name only a few. John Phillip Sousa's brass band was among the many musical bookings. Theater parties came from nearby towns — Alden, Ackley, Dows, Eldora, Hampton — often in specially chartered trains. The exterior of the building is pure Renaissance Classical. The circular entrance is called an archivolt, each bull's-eye window is an oculus, and the decorations above the flanking windows are not merely caps, but crowns. Today the Metropolitan is a movie theater.

Council Bluffs - 201 S. Third - c. 1902. This house combines a Colonial Revival elevation with a set of Neo-Classical columns. On balance, the design leans toward the Colonial side of the equation.

misnomer is based on the idea that the founding fathers were the first Americans to build houses fronted with white columns. The fact is that only a handful of Colonial houses are known to have sported a Classical portico. If it is necessary to peg the 1893 resurgence of Classicism to an American precedent, it makes more sense to call it the Greek Revival Revival. Even the President's House in Washington did not get the first of its white columns until 1824, long after the end of America's Colonial period.

The designers of Chicago's White City were not thinking about American architecture at all. They were thinking about Andrea Palladio and the Italian Renaissance of the 16th century. Which is not to say that there was no Colonial Revival. The recycling of Colonial forms began in the 1880s, was taken up with some enthusiasm about 1900, and made a big hit from 1910 to 1930. Some of the designs produced during the Neo-Classical vogue of 1895-1910 were based on the side-gabled Colonial box with attic dormer windows. The fitting out of the box might include either a Queen Anne porch or a set of columns supporting a second-story walkout. What-ever hybrid you liked best, the obligatory element was a coat of white paint.

The greatest legacy of the 1893 Colombian Exposition, and the most deplorable, was the 80-year reign of

white paint. White lead was the primary pigment of the 1830's Greek Revival, but when the picturesque styles took over, pattern-book authors lectured their readers about the inappropriateness of white. It was "no color at all" they said, and should be strictly avoided. The White City changed the rules, so that until the 1970s the resplendent Victorian palette was all but forgotten.

Cedar Rapids - Blake Blvd. and Forest Drive S.E. - 1903. Originally located close to the business district, this home was slated to be torn down in 1928. The central staircase was removed so that the house could be cut in half and moved. It was towed by horses during the day and by a street car at night. The dismembered structure was eventually reassembled two miles away.

Charles City - 305 N. Jackson - c. 1903. Here's another hybrid. Colonial elements include a gambrel roof with pedimented dormers, balustered railings, dentil-like indentations under the eaves, side-facing pilasters at the entrance, and small engaged columns at the corners. The conical spikes are a mystery.

American Foursquare *The Unadorned Successor*

Des Moines - 1128 22nd Street - c. 1898-1902. The American Foursquare represents the transitional moment when ornament was finally abolished and freeform composition was replaced with the uniformity we take to be modern.

The last product of the Victorian Age was a house so unassuming that no one thought to give it a label. It was almost square, had a wide front porch, evenly spaced windows, and a single dormer in a pyramidal roof. In 1982 the *Old House Journal* decided that this ubiquitous form was a "style orphan" that needed a proper name. Because it looked like a cube and often had four rooms on each floor, the magazine dubbed it the *American Foursquare*.

Who pioneered it and when is an abiding mystery. Historians say that none of these houses existed in 1890, but that by 1900 there were hundreds, perhaps thousands to be seen on farmsteads and town streets. The obvious idea was to build a plain, unadorned house with no pretensions at all. Anyone might have come up with it, and it seems that almost everyone did.

The structural antecedents of the Foursquare are not hard to identify. The four-planed hipped roof was used in Colonial America from the late 1600s on. If a house was wider than it was deep, the roof planes formed a ridge, but if the footprint was square the surfaces met at a common point. Later, one of the standard formats of the Italianate house was a simple cube with a shallow pyramidal roof.

Foursquare builders might have thought they were using a traditional form, but it really does not take much imagination to reinvent the cube. The virtue of a square footprint is that it yields the maximum interior floor space relative to the circumference of the walls.

In 1903 several manufacturers began prefabricating complete houses and shipping them in crates. The Radford and Alladin companies were first on the scene, followed by Sears & Roebuck in 1908. All featured Foursquares in their catalogs for more than twenty years. In

Cedar Rapids - 1536 3rd Ave. S.E.
This Foursquare has gained a Painted Ladies color scheme that, though not authentic, seems perfectly appropriate.

1926, Sears identified its designs as the Fullerton, Americus, Gladstone, Langston, Woodland, Albion, Garfield, and Rockford. Most were 24 by 26 feet, though some were as large as 30 by 36. Choices were not limited to those in the catalogs, however. Almost every local home builder could draw a set of Foursquare plans to suit a buyer's preferences.

The Foursquare is really not a style per se, but rather a type. If the edge of the roof is close to the wall, and particularly if there are round Tuscan columns holding up the porch, real estate agents are likely to list it as a Colonial. But if the roof extends well beyond the walls, and if the porch piers are thick boxes, the product may be advertised as an example of the Prairie Style.

The Foursquare was introduced just as the decorative Victorian styles were sputtering to a halt. In many ways it represents the transitional moment when ornament was finally abolished and freeform composition was replaced with the uniformity we take to be modern. As plain and unpretentious as the Foursquare is, there is something undeniably appealing about its symmetrical proportions. It looks strong and solid, dignified, not fussy, handsome instead of pretty. The Foursquare is not any sort of confection, it's just a good old-fashioned house.

Des Moines - 690 31st Street - 1906.
Adding a gabled roof to the Foursquare box created another style orphan, so labelers of our day usually call it the Homestead Style.

Cedar Falls - 903 Washington Street - c. 1905. When a Foursquare is unusually large and features a bit more of the Colonial influence, it is sometimes called American Squareframe Classic.

Des Moines - 2842 Rutland - c. 1905.

Carroll - 1004 N. Carroll Street - 1912.

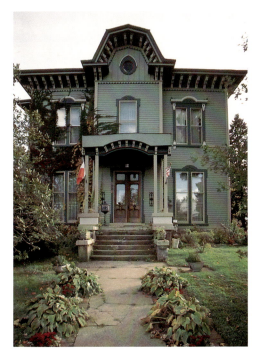

Dubuque - 890 W. 3rd Street - 1879. About 1910 this 15-room house was divided into four apartments. Of the seven original fireplaces, five remain. The renovators, who began work in 1986, say: "We have a real feeling that we are curators, not just owners."

The Renovators

The OVERSIZE LOAD banner hanging from the front porch of the Foursquare duplex was the ultimate understatement. The house it adorned was 37 feet wide, weighed 80 tons, and rested on 32 tires. Behind it in the alley was a lofty Queen Anne house of equally imposing proportions.

At the stroke of midnight Alan crashed a bottle of champagne over an undercarriage I-beam, the Mack trucks rumbled to life, and $100,000 worth of elevated real estate rolled out onto Forest Avenue in Des Moines. Strings of Christmas lights draped around the houses added a festive touch, though their purpose was to help workers judge clearances past trees and poles.

Slowly the houses rounded the corner onto 25th Street, roof shingles brushing the limbs of tall oak trees. A workman in an elevated bucket dropped a power line to the ground and TV screens went dark in nearby apartments. People wandered out onto their balconies and gaped at the houses rolling by. Most agreed it was a better spectacle than whatever they had been watching. A half-hour later the houses made it safely across the freeway bridge as passing motorists honked congratulations.

As the houses made the final turn onto 20th Street in Sherman Hill, dozens of people lined the sidewalks to greet them. Cameras flashed in the darkness. Sleepy children rubbed their eyes and pointed in amazement.

There was one last obstacle. The edge of the Foursquare's roof was blocked by a large tree limb. Someone scrambled up with a chainsaw. We hated to see the limb fall, but at least trees still grow on our streets. Antique houses do not.

A bulldozer had cut holes in the hillside and the air was filled with the aroma of freshly turned earth. The houses were lowered onto cribs made of crosshatched railroad ties. In the weeks ahead, plumb lines would be dropped, and new foundations would be built up to reach the walls.

At 3:00 AM we breathed a sigh of relief. Two more of the historic district's vacant lots had been infilled with dispossessed architecture. The hill was richer for it, even if the schemers were a bit poorer. More champagne was produced. In the middle of the night the bubbly tasted especially sweet, perhaps because the effort to save these historic houses had nearly failed.

On April 23, 1991, two weeks before the deadline, a thief broke into the Queen Anne house and stole the ornate mantelpiece. The prospective owner lost heart and abandoned the venture. Meanwhile the board of the Sherman Hill Association, which had considered moving the Foursquare, voted not to risk limited financial resources. Three smaller houses had already been exported to other neighborhoods, but the two most valuable structures on the site of Drake University's new basketball arena had no place to go.

The next morning I met Penny Schiltz and Alan Billyard, longtime Sherman Hill renovators. We signed documents to create a non-profit corporation, then went to a bank to ask for a line of credit. I wrote a check to seed the account and a sympathetic loan officer issued second mortgages on several of Penny's rental properties. The house mover's fee would be $48,000, but the cost of foundations and repairs had not been closely figured. Would the selling prices cover our costs? Maybe not.

Reporters asked why neighborhood activists were going to such extraordinary lengths to save a few houses when 65 others were headed for the scrap heap. We replied that affordable housing is a valuable resource. This was an opportunity to demonstrate our commitment.

There was also a recycling angle. Relocation of five houses saved landfill space that is now in short supply and preserved the value of 330 tons of brick, wood, shingles, plaster, nails, glass, plumbing, and wiring. It was a sermon

May 1991. Two 80-ton houses were moved seven blocks south and six blocks east.

Des Moines - 721-723 20th Street. The lot was cut down to street level so that a foundation could be constructed below the elevated frame.

Original Site. The Foursquare duplex stood for nearly 80 years in the 1400 block of 26th Street.

of a sort, but only the choir was listening.

Two months later, Penny found the stolen mantel wearing a $1,600 price tag in a Valley Junction antique shop. Police watched as she and Ray carried the mantel out and put it in their truck. Before the episode was over, a house prowler had his probation revoked and went back to jail.

The phenomenon of "urban mining" is familiar to inner-city residents. Thieves descend on boarded-up houses and bash holes in walls to get at the copper plumbing. Banisters, newel posts, doors, light fixtures, knobs and hinges – all are quickly gone. Once the house has been stripped of its "fabric," even the staunchest renovators are daunted.

It may come as a surprise to some that Des Moines, Iowa, a city with a population of less than 200,000, has its share of big-city problems. We do. The raw numbers are proportionately smaller than those of the high-population places, but the dynamics of urban angst are precisely the same.

Before deciding to move houses to Sherman Hill, we surveyed the area close to the original site. Des Moines' planographic maps, drawn from 1958 aerial photographs, showed that one nearby block originally had 22 houses, but now only 14 remained. The eight missing houses had been cash-flowed into oblivion by absentee landlords and demolished at the taxpayers' expense.

To survive, old houses must have market value, not just nostalgic or aesthetic appeal, and in the old neighborhoods where they exist the real estate is perpetually undervalued. The agent's axiom – location, location, location – often makes the salvation of an old house a risky proposition. Even though it would cost more to move houses a mile to the Sherman Hill Historic District, the market there would sustain them into the next century.

In Iowa's capital city the official "Neighborhood Revitalization" effort began in 1990 when the city and county each pledged a million dollars a year to promote renewed investment in "transitional" neighborhoods. Individual families were already working to reclaim the city's tattered streets, and many of the renovators had very little money. They often chose the worst house on the block, because that was where the greatest sweat equity could be earned.

The renovation of historic buildings may seem like an entirely new phenomenon, but the preservation movement in America has actually been reinvented at intervals over the past 150 years. Consider the following observation.

"There is an old-world expression about these venerable buildings which recommend them to our interest as historical reminiscences. And it must be confessed that there is a truth and solidity about their construction which we look for in vain in the architecture of a later day. Undoubtedly they fairly express the solid energy, determination, and great-heartedness of the founders of a new empire in the wilderness."

This was written by an author who was looking back at the architecture of a previous century. But it was penned in 1863 by architect H.H. Holly, and the buildings he was referring to were the Colonial houses of his ancestors.

The 20th century movement was mounted in 1966 when a special committee on historic preservation was impaneled by the U.S. Conference of Mayors. The committee's report, funded by the Ford Foundation, was titled *With Heritage So Rich*.

"In the past two decades more than half of the 12,000 buildings in the Historic American Buildings Survey have been demolished. Americans are increasingly aware that destruction of

Des Moines - 704 19th Street - c. 1881-84. Late Italianate elements are blended with Queen Anne wall shingles. Twenty years ago this house was in an advanced state of deterioration. Almost everything you see is new.

Des Moines - 696 18th Street - c. 1894. The Sherman Hill Association conducts annual tours called "Doors to the Past."

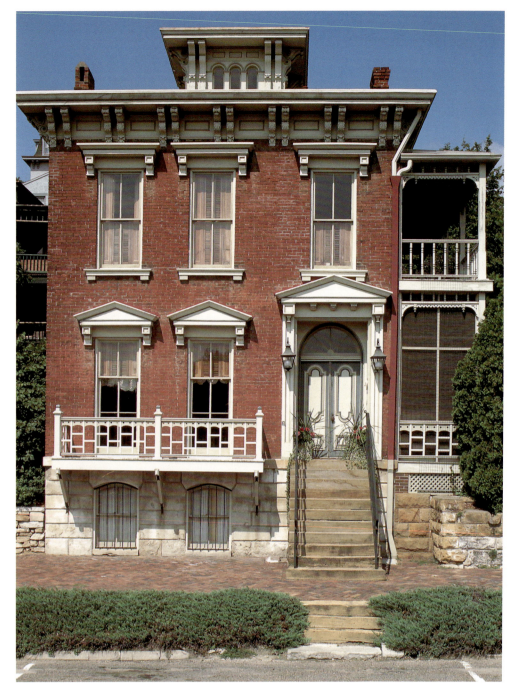

Burlington - 516 Washington Street. Some documents claim that these brick walls were built in 1845, that Abe Lincoln made a speech from the original balcony, and that the Italianate decor was added later. A competing theory holds that this house replaced an earlier structure sometime in the 1870s. One thing is certain – in the 1970s it was reduced to a burned out shell. Dedicated renovators rebuilt it from the ground up.

source of its memories, is to break the perpetual partnership that makes for orderly growth in the life of a society."

In 1966 this landmark volume stood alone on the shelves, while a host of other works focused on the disintegrating socio-political environment. The words "urban crisis" began showing up in books and magazine articles. Cities, they said, were becoming unlivable.

The instinctive response to the impoverishment of the cities was to bulldoze vast tracts of devalued housing. The plausible excuse was that the plight of the urban poor could only be remedied by destroying the slum habitat. Old buildings were the enemy.

The juggernaut of "urban renewal" was launched in the 1950s, but much of the groundwork had been laid by earlier government surveys. In 1940 the Federal Home Loan Bank Board published *Waverly – A Study in Neighborhood Conservation*. Waverly was an inner-city neighborhood of Baltimore that was then at risk of becoming a slum.

Shenandoah - 207 University Avenue. A Mansard-capped cottage is shown in the process of getting a well-deserved fixup.

our physical heritage from the past is an irrevocable loss, one which grows in its intensity with the passage of time."

In the book's introductory essay, Sidney Hyman wrote:

"A nation can be a victim of amnesia. It can lose the memories of what it was, and thereby lose the sense of what it is or wants to be. It can say it is being 'progressive' when it rips up the tissues which visibly bind one strand of its history to the next. It can say it is only getting rid of 'junk' in order to make room for the modern. What it often does instead, once it has lost the graphic

"Blight starts with the neglect of a single property and the occupance of that property by a family which has a living standard below that of the balance of the community. Gradually it begins to spread; slowly it widens and deepens; finally, from this single point of infection, it produces a full-blown slum. Each year community corrosion thus takes a terrific national toll in investment and human values…

"The Federal Home Loan Bank Board has gathered a large volume of data on the trend of residential neighborhoods in some 230 cities in the United States and has incorporated this information in detailed, confidential "security area maps." …They clearly indicate the alarming extent to which neighborhood decay has affected America's cities."

The study pointed a finger at the "undesirable classes" who were lacking in "civic values." Like a rotten apple that spoils a barrel, these nameless people were unwittingly responsible for the downward spiral of values that "robbed" homeowners of "their savings." Oddly, nothing was said about the absentee landlords in whose hands the old buildings met their ends.

To divide houses into cubbyhole apartments, wooden stairways were

Iowa City - 538 S. Gilbert - 1874. After the county sold this house at auction in 1980, renovators rebuilt the missing cupola and repaired decades of deterioration. The Italianate survivor is now a fashionable business address.

Waukon - 23 E. Main Street - c. 1865-1875. This limestone house is one of the few Octagons built after the Civil War. The original cupola and porch were removed about 1910, but new ones were built during a renovation that lasted from 1983 to 1991.

Mount Pleasant - 500 W. Monroe - c. 1894. A sign posted on one of the temporary timbers shows that the renovation work is funded in part by a REAP grant from the state of Iowa. REAP stands for Resource Enhancement and Protection. To qualify for a subsidy, a building must be eligible for the National Register of Historic Places.

attached to the sides so that private entrances could be cut through second-floor walls. These cancerous exoskeletons were the first signs of impending decay. Just as fossil fuel is burned to release stored energy, old buildings were routinely disinvested to release stored equity.

At the time of the FHLB study, the remodeling of old housing stock was the principal strategy, so drawings were included to show what could be done. The planners proposed to take an 1870 house, replace the Mansard roof with a Colonial one, add dormer windows, a pediment over the door, and a columned entrance where the porch had been. The idea was to make the inner city look like a new suburb.

Ten years later this idea must have seemed ludicrous, because the plan that was adopted, again relying on confidential security maps, was to clear-cut the old neighborhoods and turn the vacant land over to commercial development. With the Housing Act of 1949, the federal government began paying two-thirds of the demolition "write down." By 1968 the federal subsidy was nearly a billion dollars a year. When reporters were not around to quote them, urban planners called the new strategy "negro removal."

The prevailing attitude about slum creation had been clearly enunciated in the FHLB's 1940 study.

"The general attitude toward it – perhaps because of its almost imperceptible advance – has always been one of patient acquiescence in a natural but impersonal phenomenon, which cannot be controlled but need not be feared."

The 1950's acquiescence required the "red lining" of neighborhoods so that mortgage lenders could create new slums. It worked.

By the early 1970s a fresh set of values was emerging. The clarion call came from San Francisco, where an entire community of Victorian homes – 5,000 redwood-framed houses – was systematically destroyed. The process was abruptly halted in 1974 by an "outraged citizenry."

The new preservation movement was best chronicled by Richard Ernie Reed in his 1979 book *Return To The City*.

"We are coming home again for more than good, cheap shelter, which many of the deteriorated old structures provide in abundance. We are coming home again for an almost extinct sense of quality… We left the city, worn out, shabby, smelling of old ways and hard times. We slipped out of it like one shrugs off an old coat, leaving it to lie in a heap… But in spite of what seems like a continuing migration from the cities, a countermigration seems to be beginning. A new kind of American

Forest City - 516 N. Clark Street. Reconstruction of the porch is one of the most common renovation projects.

West Des Moines - 2001 Fuller Road - c. 1850. Builder James Jordan and his wife Cynthia were staunch Methodists who made their home a stop on the Underground Railroad. Because the secrets of these clandestine outposts were closely guarded, no one knows how many escaping slaves were hidden in or near the house. It is known that famed abolitionist John Brown stopped here shortly before his raid on the U.S. Arsenal at Harpers Ferry, Virginia in October 1859. Italianate brackets and vernacular porch decorations were added about 1870 when the building was enlarged and remodeled. The Jordan House was acquired in 1978 by the West Des Moines Historical Society, and most of the restoration work was completed in time for the 1993 Valley Junction Centennial. It is now a public museum.

Des Moines - E. 6th and Grand Avenue - 1878. The Studio Building is an 87-foot front divided into stores. In 1922 the original window caps were chiseled off so that the walls could be modernized with concrete panels. In 1996 the owner restored the original appearance with new caps made of fiberglass-reinforced concrete. The authentic design was copied from old photographs and from a nearby building that employed the same style.

with a new kind of attitude is coming back to the city to clean the dust of disuse and repair the damage of ill-use from many old structures… The urban pioneers, like their earlier namesakes, have to struggle and take risks for what they believe in. The wilderness of the city holds promise, but it also holds fear…

"It is expensive to keep up an old house. It takes a certain depth of commitment we aren't usually required to give: Hundreds of dusty hours of cleaning, painting, sanding, and sawing; thousands of dollars spent for the professional help which is beyond our skills. If the assessor or accountant measured the old houses' eroded foundations with his rule of 'economic feasibility,' very few old structures would be left standing. An old building is restored more from the heart than the head and, usually, only later does the head discover that the heart was right all along."

While the renovators were gaining a foothold in the urban centers, others were searching for a quieter way of life in the small towns. Old houses there had not suffered the same indignities as those of the city. Most had not been carved into cramped apartments, with showers installed in closets, they had merely been forgotten. The searchers could buy more house for a dollar with whatever money they had, but in Iowa's small towns a different problem was encountered – a lack of jobs.

Of the state's 953 incorporated municipalities, 93% have populations of less than 5,000. These rural towns once served as retail centers and shipping terminals for legions of small-acreage farmers. For most of this century their populations remained stable, but in the 1980s nearly 70% of Iowa's towns lost population and 20% of the retail businesses closed. It was too easy for shoppers to get in their cars and zip off to Sioux City, Ottumwa, Cedar Rapids, Davenport, or Des Moines. If you walked around the parking lot of an urban shopping mall on a weekend, you could spot license plates from dozens of Iowa counties. Soon corn fields along interstate highways were paved over to

Jefferson - 1898. This is probably Iowa's largest surviving metal-clad building. Original store windows have been replaced with modern brick.

build rural outlet malls.

There were enough urban expatriates and stalwart small-town natives to preserve the best Victorian houses, but for most of the 1980s the old commercial buildings continued to languish. The Main Street renaissance was the wind that turned the tide.

The *Main Street* concept was launched in 1977 by the National Trust for Historic Preservation to help towns "map out a prosperous future by breathing new economic life into neglected commercial districts."

"Rather than tearing down the old buildings and starting from scratch, the National Main Street Center believes the future of your commercial district lies in making the most of its past. We'll help you recognize and reclaim the architectural gems that once made your Main Street a source of pride and that can once again give it a distinct marketing edge."

In 1985 the Iowa Legislature appropriated funds for Main Street Iowa, a four-part program that emphasizes community organization, promotion, design quality, and business improvement. It was "founded on the goal of economic development within the context of historic preservation."

Very little of the work was done by state employees. Instead, thousands of volunteer hours were donated by residents in each of the 39 participating towns. The 1996 Ten Year Report listed a net gain of 1,303 businesses, 3,560 jobs, and nearly $122 million in private investment, all leveraged with only $3.6 million in government funds. During this ten year period, 2,905 buildings were renovated.

Iowa's small towns are now a living museum of restored buildings – from Painted Lady bed-and-breakfast inns to indigenous one-of-a-kind retail outlets. Each is a work of art that speaks to us not of a bygone era, but of a new period in American history. If it needed proving, Iowa has certainly proved it. Historic preservation is good business.

Tipton - 610 Lynn Street - 1905. The towered Queen Anne Style lingered into the early years of the 20th century, gradually surrendering its decorative details.

Painted Ladies   *Ebullient Celebration of Rediscovered Charm*

The *Colorist Movement* began in San Francisco in the late 1960s. Some think that a group of hippies sharing a Western Addition commune grew tired of splashing psychedelic colors on VW Microbuses and turned their attention to the wooden envelope that encircled them. Serious students of the craft dismiss this hypothesis and insist that earnest historians were responsible for the fad.

The color sleuths first armed themselves with ordinary paint scrapers and razor blades, but soon resorted to polarized-light microscopes and mass spectrometers. They dissected the hidden layers of paint on their houses and figured out how the colors had been skewed by chemical decomposition. There were no color photographs to go by, and no one left alive to explain what they found, but the scientific evidence was irrefutable. Those supposedly puritanical Victorians had actually decorated their houses with lavish combinations of color ranging from the rich and sublime to the bold, playful, and jarring. Old magazine articles proved that certain 19th century colorists were reviled by their contemporaries for exceeding the bounds of good taste.

Just as today, there were two basic types of paints – oil based and water based. Michelangelo ground pigments into linseed oil, and his basic recipe lasted for five hundred years. If economy was important, the liquid was usually cow's milk, though water slaked with lime and crushed oyster shells worked reasonably well.

Nineteenth century pigments were derived from a variety of natural substances: gray from blueberries, red from clay, blue from cobalt ore, green from copper, yellow from buckthorn berries and sulfur, deep blue from scorched peach pits. Until the advent of manufactured colors, painters mixed their own pigments in front yards before getting

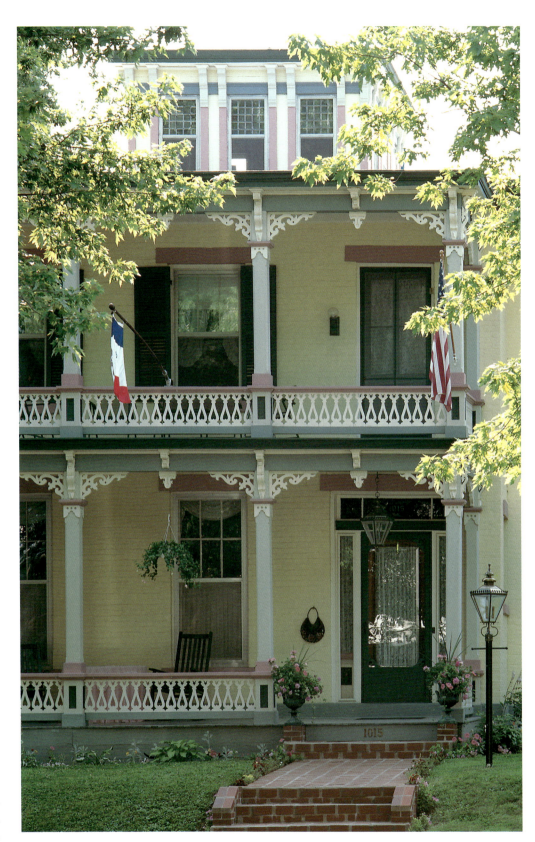

Burlington - 1015 N. 5th Street - 1859. Flat lintels above the windows, sidelights next to the door, and a boxy cupola on the roof are all clues that this house was built before the Civil War. The two-story porch appears to be a modern recreation.

These decorative details were photographed in Parkersburg and St. Ansgar. The similarity of hues suggests that the decorators were looking at the same spots on the color wheel.

out the brushes.

One of the first makers of ready-mix paint was the F.W. Devoe Company. In the late 1860s it marketed a collection of muted yellows, browns, and russets that were well suited to the prevailing Italianate and Second Empire houses. This palette gave way gradually to the more extravagant set of colors we associate with the great Painted Ladies, the massive Queen Annes.

Pattern-book architects had definite views on the proper uses of color. Most recommended using three basic paints – one for the body of the house, one for the window surrounds, and another to highlight the decorative elements. Not to be constrained by professional guidelines, homeowners reasoned that if three colors were good, seven were better. They had a lot of wooden ornament to highlight, and there were hundreds of colors from which to choose.

To understand what modern colorists are talking about, you have to learn their language. All colors begin with the *primaries* – red, blue, and yellow. When two of these are mixed to produce green, violet, or orange, the product is defined as *secondary* or *complementary*. For easy reference, these six basic colors are arranged on a wheel like numbers on a clock face. Yellow is at 12 o'clock, orange at two, red at four, violet at six, blue at eight, and green at ten o'clock, with intermediate colors occupying the odd-numbered spots on the dial.

Chroma is the intensity or saturation of a paint, while *value* defines its relative position on a light-to-dark scale. Thus, the primaries are high-chroma, gray is low-chroma, and a bright yellow has a greater value than a dark blue. Black and white are defined as *neutral* colors, so that a paint is said to be a *tint* if it is lightened with white, or a *shade* if it is darkened with black.

Now that we have all this figured out, we can begin to think about the four basic color schemes. The easiest is *monochromatic* – it's all one color. The *complementary* scheme requires that you pick two colors that are opposite each

Parkersburg - 6th and Buswell. Even the smallest of houses is a suitable canvas for the brushstrokes of today's Colorist Movement.

other on the wheel – such as yellow-orange and blue-violet. If you don't like that, go for the *triad* scheme with three colors that are equidistant on the wheel. Your last choice is the *analogous* scheme, a combination of any three adjoining spots on the wheel.

Stumped? Well, all you have to do is stroll off to the paint store and pick several of the 1600 individual colors identified by their makers with names like Sandalwood, Cranberry, and Somerset Gray. Nobody said fixing an old house was going to be easy.

Osceola - 222 W. McLane Street - c. 1907. The present owners are urban expatriates who went looking for an old house to restore. George Barber featured the plan on the cover of his first magazine in January 1895.

INDEX

MAP KEY	TOWN	PAGE(s)
1	Adel	62
2	Albia	52, 80, 81
3	Algona	30
4	Ames	34
5	Anamosa	36
6	Andrew	9, 76
7	Atlantic	115
8	Avoca	51
9	Bedford	58, 75
10	Bellevue	14, 66
11	Bentonsport	7, 8
12	Bloomfield	102
13	Bonaparte	118
14	Boone	28
15	Britt	77
16	Burlington	15, 18, 41, 132, 139
17	Carroll	113, 127
18	Cedar Falls	26, 49, 60, 127
19	Cedar Rapids	123, 126
20	Centerville	31
21	Chariton	67
22	Charles City	124
23	Clarinda	57, 63, 82, 83
24	Clarksville	119
25	Clermont	43
26	Clinton	40
27	Corning	48
28	Corydon	86
29	Council Bluffs	10, 28, 44, 52, 97, 122
30	Creston	73
31	Davenport	11, 21, 37, 64, 69, 86, 112
32	Decorah	20, 23, 27, 32
33	Des Moines	27, 33, 39, 72, 87, 100, 125, 126, 127, 130, 131, 135, 136
34	Dow City	35
35	Dubuque	16, 24, 38, 41, 42, 44, 47, 53, 56, 85, 93, 109, 128, 129
36	Eldora	91
37	Elkader	9
38	Fairfield	98, 116
39	Forest City	100, 120, 135
40	Fort Madison	10, 35, 75, 107
41	Grinnell	23, 89
42	Griswold	105
43	Grundy Center	98
44	Hampton	106
45	Harlan	82
46	Independence	33, 34, 58,
47	Indianola	35
48	Iowa City	6, 46, 59, 84, 133
49	Iowa Falls	121
50	Keokuk	17, 19, 31, 65, 109
51	Jefferson	56, 103, 137
52	Lamoni	67
53	Lansing	40
54	LeMars	71
55	Manchester	22
56	Manning	56, 81
57	Marshalltown	45, 114
58	Maquoketa	106
59	McGregor	78
60	Mechanicsville	34, 117
61	Mitchellville	68
62	Monticello	62
63	Mount Pleasant	16, 29, 43, 68, 134
64	Mount Vernon	70, 99
65	Muscatine	11, 12, 13, 24
66	New Hampton	104
67	Newton	25
68	Northwood	35
69	Onawa	70
70	Osage	48, 52
71	Osceola	96, 141
72	Oskaloosa	8, 49, 79
73	Ottumwa	30, 54
74	Parkersburg	95, 107, 140
75	Pella	32, 55, 61, 71
76	Perry	110
77	Prairie City	cover, 51, 90
78	Red Oak	53, 58, 66, 101, 113
79	Rock Rapids	76
80	Riverdale	7
81	St. Ansgar	108, 140
82	Salem	6
83	Shenandoah	132
84	Sioux City	88, 92, 94
85	Storm Lake	45
86	Tipton	74, 108, 138
87	Traer	46, 103
88	Villisca	111, 115
89	Vinton	25, 89, 99, 110
90	Washington	5, 17, 104
91	Waterloo	23, 47
92	Waukon	133
93	Wilton	57
94	Winterset	50, 69

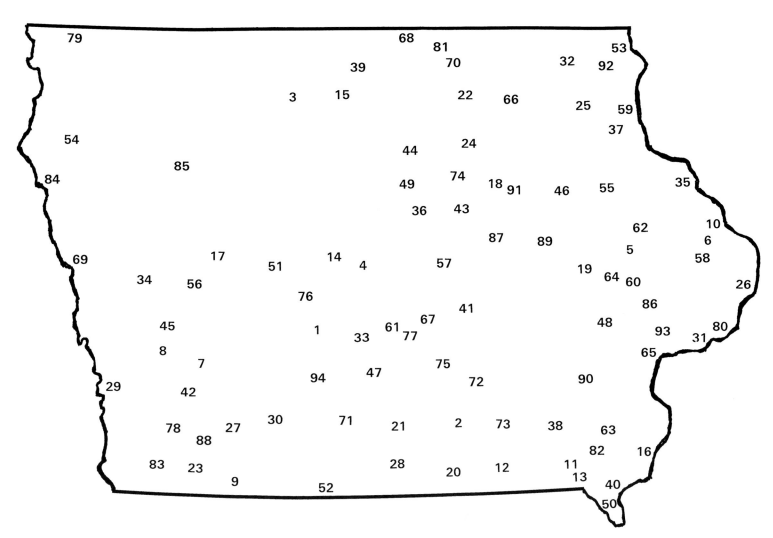

BIBLIOGRAPHY

IOWA HISTORY

I Remember I Remember by Cyrenus Cole. State Historical Society of Iowa, 1936.

Steamboating On the Upper Missippi – The Water Way to Iowa by William J. Petersen. The State Historical Society of Iowa, 1937.

Iowa Old and New by John Ely Briggs. The University Publishing Company, 1939.

Iowa Through the Years by Cyrenus Cole. State Historical Society of Iowa, 1940.

Iowa...Land of Many Mills by Jacob A. Swisher. State Historical Society of Iowa, 1940.

The Iowa Indians by Thomas P. Christensen. Laurance Press, 1954.

Iowa Beautiful Land – A History of Iowa by Jessie Merrill Dwelle. Klipto Loose Leaf Company, 1958.

Tell a Tale of Iowa by Don Doyle Brown. Wallace-Homestead Company, 1965.

Nineteenth Century Home Architecture of Iowa City by Margaret N. Keyes. University of Iowa Press, 1966.

High Points of Iowa History by Eugene N. Hastie, 1971.

A History of Iowa by Leland L. Sage. The Iowa State University Press, 1974.

The Steamboat Bertrand: History, Excavation, and Architecture by Jerome E. Petsche. National Park Service, U.S. Department of the Interior, 1974.

Terrace Hill by Scherrie Goettsch and Steve Weinberg. Wallace-Homestead Book Company, 1978.

Des Moines: Capital City by Orin L. Dahl. Continental Heritage, Inc., 1978.

Iowa – A Bicentennial History by Joseph Frazier Wall. W.W. Norton & Company, 1978.

Des Moines and Polk County – Flag on the Prairie by Barbara Beving Long. Windsor Publications, Inc, 1988.

Buildings of Iowa by David Gebhard and Gerald Mansheim. Oxford University Press, 1993.

ARCHITECTURAL STYLE

American Architecture Since 1780 – A Guide to the Styles by Marcus Whiffen. The MIT Press, 1968

The American House by Mary Mix Foley and Madelaine Thatcher. Harper & Row Publishers, 1980.

A Field Guide to American Architecture by Carole Rifkind. New American Library, 1980.

What STYLE is it? The Preservation Press, National Trust for Historic Preservation, 1983.

A Field Guide to American Houses by Virginia and Lee McAlester. Alfred Knopf, 1984.

American House Styles by John Milnes Baker. W.W. Norton & Company, 1994.

House Styles in America: The Old-House Journal Guide to the Architecture of American Homes by James C. Massey and Shirley Maxwell. Penguin Studio, 1996.

ARCHITECTURAL HISTORY

How to Know Architecture: The Human Elements in the Evolution of Styles by Frank E. Wallis. Harper and Brothers, 1910.

Domestic Gothic of the Tudor Period by Sydney E. Castle. International Casement Company, 1927.

The Story of Architecture in America by Thomas E. Tallmadge. W.W. Norton & Company, 1927.

Waverly: A Study in Neighborhood Conservation. Federal Home Loan Bank Board, 1940.

Space, Time and Architecture by Sigfried Giedion. The Harvard University Press, 1949.

The Shingle Style – Architectural Theory and Design from Richardson to the Origins of Wright by Vincent J. Scully, Jr. Yale University Press, 1955.

The Gingerbread Age by John Maass. Greenwich House, 1957.

Architecture: Nineteenth and Twentieth Centuries by Henry-Russell Hitchcock. Penguin Books, 1958.

Art And Life In America by Oliver W. Larkin. Holt, Rinehart and Winston, 1960.

Architecture In America: A Battle of Styles edited by William A. Coles and Henry Hope Reed, Jr. Appleton-Century-Crofts Inc., 1961.

The Architecture of America: A Social and Cultural History by John Burchard and Albert Bush-Brown. The Atlantic Monthly Press, 1961.

The English Tradition in Architecture by John Gloag. Barnes & Noble Inc., 1963.

Images of American Living – Four Centuries of Architecture and Furniture as Cultural Expression by Alan Gowans. J.P. Lippincott Company, 1964.

Architecture, Ambition, and Americans – A Social History of American Architecture by Wayne Andrews. The Free Press of Glencoe, 1964.

The Rise of an American Architecture by Henry-Russell Hitchcock, Albert Fein, Winston Weisman, and Vincent Scully. Praeger Publishers, 1970.

The Art-Makers of Nineteenth-Century America by Russell Lynes. Atheneum, 1970.

American Buildings and Their Architects – Technology and the Picturesque by William H. Pierson, Jr. Doubleday & Company, 1970.

The Architecture of Choice: Eclecticism in America 1880-1930 by Walter C. Kidney. George Braziller, 1974.

American Gothic by Wayne Andrews, 1975.

Richard Norman Shaw by Andrew Saint. Yale University Press, 1976.

A Choice Over Our Heads: A Guide to Architecture and Design Since 1830 by Lawrence Burton. Eastview Editions Inc., 1979.

The Victorian Country House by Mark Girouard. Yale University Press, 1979.

A Concise History of American Architecture by Leland M. Roth. Harper & Row, 1979.

The Rise of Architectural History by David Watkin. The Architectural Press, Eastview Editions Inc., 1980.

American Architecture 1607-1976 by Marcus Whiffen and Frederick Koeper. The MIT Press, 1981.

Flight of Fancy: The Banishment and Return of Ornament by Brent C. Brolin. St. Martin's Press, 1985.

The Comfortable House: North American Suburban Architecture 1890-1930 by Alan Gowans. The MIT Press, 1986.

Classical Architecture in Renaissance Europe 1419-1585 by John Fitzhugh Millar. Thirteen Colonies Press, 1987.

The Glory of the English House by Lionel Esher and Clay Perry. Bulfinch Press, 1991.

Metals in America's Historic Buildings by Margot Gayle and David W. Look. U.S. Department of the Interior, 1992.

19th CENTURY HISTORY

To Appomatotox – Nine April Days, 1865 by Burke Davis. Rinehart & Company, 1959.

The Gilded Age and After edited by John A. DeNovo. Charles Scribner's Sons, 1972.

Queen Victoria: From Her Birth to the Death of the Prince Consort by Cecil Woodham-Smith. Alfred A. Knopf, 1972.

The Rise of Industrial America by Page Smith. McGraw-Hill Book Company, 1984.

REPRINTS

Cottage Residences by Andrew Jackson Downing (1842). Dover Publications, 1981.

The Architecture of Country Houses by Andrew Jackson Downing (1850). Dover Publications, 1969.

The Model Architect by Samual Sloan (1852). Reprinted as Sloan's Victorian Buildings by Dover Publications, 1980.

Country Seats (1863) and *Modern Dwellings* (1878) by Henry Hudson Holly. The American Life Foundation, 1977.

Woodward's National Architect by George E. Woodward and Edward G. Thompson (1869). Dover Publications, 1988.

Westward by Rail: The New Route to the East by W.F. Rae (1869). Indianhead Books, 1993.

Hints on Household Taste by Charles L. Eastlake (1868). Reprint of 1878 edition by Dover Publications, 1969.

A History of the Gothic Revival by Charles L. Eastlake (1872). American Life Foundation, 1975.

Palliser's American Cottage Homes by George and Charles Palliser (1878). Dover Publications, 1990.

Modern Architectural Designs and Details by William T. Comstock (1881). Reprinted as Victorian Domestic Architectural Plans and Details by Dover Publications, 1987.

American Architecture and Other Writings by Montgomery Schuyler (1883). Harvard University Press collection, 1961.

The Mulliner Catalog of 1893 by the Mulliner Box & Planing Company. Dover Publications, 1995.

Sears, Roebuck Catalog of Houses, 1926. The Athenaeum of Philadelphia and Dover Publications, 1991.

The Brown Decades: A Study of the Arts in America by Lewis Mumford (1931). Dover Publications, 1971.

Early American Architecture by Hugh Morrison. Oxford University Press, 1952. Dover Publications, 1987.

Architectural Elements: The Technological Revolution edited by Diane S. Waite. The Pyne Press.

RENOVATION

Return To The City – How To Restore Old Buildings and Ourselves in America's Historic Urban Neighborhoods by Richard Ernie Reed. Doubleday & Company, 1979.

Old House Colors by Lawrence Schwin III. Sterling Publishing Company, 1990.

How To Create Your Own Painted Lady by Elizabeth Pomada and Michael Larsen. E.P. Dutton, 1989.

PERIODICALS

The Palimpsest. The Iowa State Historical Department, Division of the State Historical Society.

The Iowan. The Iowan, Inc. a division of Mid-America Publishing Corporation.

The Old-House Journal.